D1522757

LARRY FAULKNER, CFEI &
MICHELLE BOHLS LMFT, FAGPA

FROM MONEY DISASTER TO PROSPERITY

THE
<u>BREAKTHROUGH</u>
FORMULA

Published by
Faulkner Financial Freedom

This publication is designed to provide competent and reliable information regarding the subject matter covered. However, it is sold with the understanding that the author and publisher are not engaged in rendering legal, financial, or other professional advice. The mention of interest rates and other financial examples are merely that—examples. We provide no guarantee that your results would be the same as the illustrative examples contained in this text. Laws and practices often vary from state to state and country to country, and if legal or other expert assistance is required, the services of a professional should be sought. The author and publisher specifically disclaim any liability that is incurred from the use or application of the contents of this book.

ISBN: 9798465861632

Cover Designed by Tim Barber
Illustrations by Douglas Brown, albumartist.com
Interior designed by Danielle H. Acee, authorsassistant.com

This book is dedicated to those who struggle mightily and overcome the formidable obstacles that block their path to their best destiny!

Hardships often prepare ordinary people for extraordinary destiny.

—C. S. Lewis

Table of Contents

My Story

D o you think one book could change the course of your life? A book changed the course and direction of my life many years ago. It certainly interrupted my self-destructive fast-track to living a life filled with perpetual misery. In fact, that book might even have saved my life.

I am a police officer who became a self-made millionaire. I achieved this goal by learning to recognize the barriers that held me back. After recognizing them, I learned to overcome them. The barriers were actually roadblocks that created self-destructive behaviors that sabotaged my efforts to achieve my goals. These may be problems you've encountered on your journey to your own goals. Dealing with your life problems is a critical part of the Breakthrough Formula for Prosperity. Of course, goal setting and increasing your financial knowledge are also important, but these elements are by far the easier parts of the success formula.

To give you the full context and understanding of why my story is important to you, we need to go back to when I was a teenager—somewhere around 14 to 15 years of age. At that young age, I was already smoking cigarettes while hanging out with my friends. Those behaviors soon led to smoking marijuana with these same friends. Sometimes we would all get together and skip school, smoke marijuana and drink alcohol, which was surprisingly easy for teens to get back then. I can remember trying to sober up before we went home to our parents. We were so young we couldn't drive, so we had to walk everywhere, which was helpful in that process. At school, I was performing poorly. I purposefully only did the bare minimum I needed to pass each class, and I was barely advancing to each grade. Lying about nearly everything to everyone was my daily routine.

As I think back, I can remember almost being addicted to the thrill of taking risks and surviving them or avoiding the consequences of my actions. It was almost like a drug! I often thought, *What crazy thing can I get away with today?* I damaged property and did crazy stunts just for the thrill of doing them. Before I was old enough to even drive a car, I did things with my friends I would be ashamed to admit today. The thrill of those risks seemed to grant me relief from my stressful life.

I now know that many of the decisions I was making those many years ago were likely made because I had suffered significant, life-threatening emotional events as a child from my less-than-ideal home life and upbringing. As many children who have experienced a physically and mentally abusive childhoods do, I was acting out and engaged in an entire array of behaviors that could land me in serious trouble, negatively impact my health or seriously damage my future chances at success. Again, this is a very common story and is in no way unique. Millions of other children who had a painful childhood have very similar stories.

What saved me was one of my more positive hobbies. I liked to read. I read quite a bit because it helped me escape mentally from the physical and mental abuse of my unhappy home life, and one book saved me from almost certain ruin. I read plenty of trash, of course, but I also read many great classical works and nonfiction as well. One day, when I was a freshman in high school, my father brought home *How to Win Friends and Influence People* by Dale Carnegie.[1] He was attempting to read it, but mostly it just sat around our house. I picked it up, and I ended up devouring it. I learned that Mr. Carnegie believed you could achieve life satisfaction, happiness, and financial success by setting goals and taking directed actions to achieve those goals.

This book and its positive message of self-determination had a significant influence upon my life both then and now. Self-determination, abundant financial resources and creating allies all seemed like superb ideas to me, especially given my home situation. I was thrilled with the concept that I could be the captain of my own life—a better life where I could choose my outcomes. I was also deeply captivated by envisioning a financial result and then going out and achieving it.

If you are now struck by the dichotomy of the fact that I would do so little of my assigned schoolwork and then go home and happily read copious amounts on my own, you would not be alone. My parents and teachers noticed this as well and commented frequently and negatively about it. The consensus back then was that I "lacked proper motivation." My father tried many times, to no avail, to supply me with the proper motivation by beating me black and blue. I now understand that it was likely these many experiences that produced my inner belief that I was "not good enough." This belief and my behaviors to prove him right held me back in my early life.

My story is particularly important because of how everything changed. As a young man, I began to feel like my behavior did not reflect who I was at my core and certainly not who I wanted to be in the future. I wanted to achieve things. I wanted to be successful! I wanted to be rich! I also wanted to help people, not be destructive.

With those newfound goals in mind, I started to feel very uneasy about my life choices as I began my junior year in high school. Then my unease turned into anxiety. What the heck was I doing? Where was I headed? What was my current behavior going to get me? Of course, I knew the answer was nothing good, and I was headed nowhere I wanted to go. I began to crave something more from my life. Even though I had read the Carnegie book a year or so earlier, it occupied my thoughts. I created a vision in my mind of what I wanted, and I began a campaign to bring this vision into reality. I stopped skipping school with my friends, I started doing my schoolwork, I made different friends, and I started obtaining mostly A's in my high school classes. I stopped smoking marijuana, I stopped drinking alcohol while I was underage, I got a part-time job, and I purposefully and intentionally altered my life trajectory. I became successful in achieving all the goals I set. I soon realized that just as making poor decisions created poor outcomes, setting goals, and making good decisions created great outcomes.

I graduated high school and began working while going to college part time. This continued until I finally started a career at the local police department, which is a goal I set in high school. I made pretty good money for the southern Ohio area. No path is ever smooth or problem free, but I succeeded beyond my initial vision, both in my career and in my education. I eventually graduated with honors and a master's degree in evidence-based policing at the University of Cincinnati.

Creating wealth was one of several goals I set back in high school. After I met my wife, we made this a shared goal. Again, there were many bumps in the road, but we were eventually successful with our finances, even while raising three growing boys. In fact, we crushed our goals and have now set new ones.

My wife and I became self-made millionaires in less than 25 years! I can still remember the moment we discovered that we had smashed through the million-dollar-net-worth barrier. While visiting our son, daughter-in-law, and granddaughter in Virginia, we were reviewing our monthly budget numbers and our investment results. Our investment accounts had hovered well below the million-dollar mark for months, stuck in a virtual quagmire. Then, all at once, big gains occurred, as is often the case in financial markets. We not only reached the million-dollar mark, but we found that we had surpassed it and had moved comfortably beyond our long-cherished goal.

We both sat in stunned silence, each lost in thought. Finally, my wife said, "Congratulations, Mr. Faulkner."

"Congratulations, Ms. Faulkner!" I replied. Then, we held each other tightly for a long time while each of us thought about our bright future ahead after achieving our long-held dream. I was also thinking about our journey and how we'd arrived at that moment. It meant we both had real freedom for the rest of our lives, which is a very precious thing!

After achieving our goal, I began to notice something very strange. My peers, who made as much money or even more than I did, were always broke. In fact, most of my fellow officers were in dire financial straits. Being broke was not only common among my police peers who were making great wages but also among nurses, police chiefs, lawyers, doctors and even executives making a whopping $300k to $350k per year! In fact, some could not afford to buy a simple meal and usually had to skip eating lunch during their workdays.

Many of my friends and coworkers lived in quiet, secret desperation because of their money issues. We noticed our friends rarely ever talked about their money problems because of the shame our society puts on those who are unsuccessful in handling money. Their shame kept them feeling alone, which compounded their problems. I wondered about their life situations or beliefs they had that were preventing them from managing their financial resources effectively. Perhaps they'd internalized money stories (also called money scripts) such as:

- Money is bad and I want to avoid it.
- I can always make more money later.
- I will live forever.
- Life is short, so I might as well enjoy my money.
- You can never get rich doing this job.

Our friends and peers were not foolish people. They were smart in every other area of their lives. They were good, kind, considerate people we were proud to call our friends. Yet, their financial lives were absolute disasters. Even though they made plenty of money, they all owed more than they made because they succumbed to a myriad of financially sabotaging behaviors and habits.

My wife and I wanted our children, extended family, and our friends to experience the same type of success we'd had. We raised three boys to become financially responsible adults, and we began coaching others (usually our friends) in the area of financial wellness. Additionally, I took it a step further and began instructing basic, intermediate, and advanced financial education classes, which I've continued doing over the last dozen or so years.

The lesson from my story is that I was able to motivate myself into a new way of thinking. It was not an easy task for me, and I don't assume it is for others. You must first handle the most pressing problems in your life, then you must educate yourself on how and what must be done before you can begin working toward your goals. But, if a 16-year-old kid can do it, I truly believe others can as well. The question you must ask yourself now is, are you willing to read this book to learn the Breakthrough Formula for Prosperity and how this formula could improve your life? I'm certain that if you can be open to the concepts in this book, you can use them to create a positive difference in your future.

Chapter 1
From Money Disaster to Breakthrough Prosperity

How would you complete the sentences below?

Money is _____.
Debt is _____.
Rich people are _____.

Are any of these beliefs holding you back from financial success?

I met Theresa a few years back. She was a supervisor at a local restaurant working the early-morning shift. I saw her most mornings when I would stop in to pick up a diet soda (we all have our vices in life). After a while, we became friends. From our previous discussions, Theresa knew I taught financial classes at our local jail for prisoners trying to rebuild their lives. One day, she shared with me that she had been addicted to crystal methamphetamine. She spent all the money she had—and some money she didn't have—on this drug. She was eventually arrested and had served many months in the same jail I was now teaching in. When she was released, she had an extensive drug recovery period before returning home to be reunited with her children.

She was a supervisor at the restaurant and was making reasonably decent money. She was very grateful for her new life of sobriety and had repaired most of her relationships she'd damaged during her addiction. Feeling empowered with her renewed lease on life and stability at home, she was now interested in starting her own business and needed some technical business training referrals—which I was happy to provide her.

Theresa's story is not unusual. People have gone to prison, many of them drug addicted, with pasts so horrible you can't even imagine the memories they carry around with them. When they were incarcerated, their personal and professional lives were destroyed. Yet, after being released, they managed to overcome their various problems and rebuild their lives.

Theresa grew up with her mom and their home life was always in chaos. Her mom moved around a lot and lived with many different men during Theresa's childhood. The relationships her mother built with these men never seemed to last long. From Theresa's perspective, her mom didn't seem to have a lot of time for her. I believe this led Theresa to struggle with feelings of low self-worth.

Theresa quit her job at the restaurant a month after I gave her the information and went on to start her business in another area of the state. As of today, she is doing great mentally and physically and is still working on her business dreams. She has a long-term relationship with a significant other who understands her past, accepts it, and still believes in her. They are committed to a long-term relationship and raising a blended family. She's come a long way from the county jail. Theresa is one of the success stories I've included to show it is possible to go from being in a money disaster and living in misery to creating a new life of prosperity and serenity. *(See workbook section for other inspiring stories.)*

What is a money disaster?

- You do not have enough money to pay your bills.
- You always feel like you don't have enough money to take care of yourself.
- You are likely in significant debt.
- You might also be suffering from a lack of clarity regarding your money, such as how much money you actually have, where your money is or where your money is going.
- You have shame surrounding your lack of money success.

Here is a radical concept I intend to prove in this chapter and throughout the rest of this book that applies directly to what may be holding you back from the success you desire:

> *The reason you may have not been successful in managing your finances is because your past negative childhood experiences have secretly sabotaged you. Past negative experiences or traumas create unconscious, negative feelings and emotions, which in turn create self-defeating financial behaviors and habits.*

Even though this may seem like an "excuse," it is absolutely true! Your self-sabotaging behaviors and habits are creating unseen boundaries you haven't yet managed to cross.

At this point, we can't go much further without also defining childhood trauma for the purposes of this book:

> *Childhood trauma is defined as an experience that overwhelms a child's psyche and/or nervous system during the childhood developmental stages of life.*

> *It is perceived as a life-threatening event to the child (whether or not it actually is), or the child witnesses it happen to someone else the child cares about—like a family member.*

As a child, you can be overwhelmed pretty easily by various negative, emotionally charged events. When the psyche and nervous system are overwhelmed, they create stress-induced, limiting beliefs about yourself that are buried deep within your subconscious—even down to a cellular level in your body.[1] These beliefs are harmful because subconsciously they negatively influence all of our behaviors or internal self-beliefs. Some examples of these self-beliefs include:

- I don't deserve to be happy.
- I am weak.
- I am powerless.
- I am not good enough.
- It is all my fault.
- Weak people don't deserve good things.

Even though your conscious mind knows all of these beliefs are not true, your subconscious mind, your body, your programing or whatever you call it believes these self-defeating statements to absolutely be true! So even though your conscious mind says, "I am going to manage my money well," your programing says, "I am inadequate and not worthy of a good life." These subconscious thoughts caused by childhood traumas on your developing mind created unconscious, limiting beliefs that are still influencing your behavior today. These limiting beliefs can remain reasonably persistent throughout life, unless you take action to alter them.

Some of you have struggled with this problem in the past and tried to solve it without much success. I know others have hurt you, maybe even badly. I know you have tried to move on and progress past this pain, yet this hurt lingers like a toothache. Others may have made it clear to you they don't believe in you or have no faith in you. They are wrong! Even if no one else does, I have faith in your ability to change if that is what you choose! Your past financial failures stem from a lack of understanding of the root causes of the problems you are now facing. It is not your fault!

Life change begins by first altering the way you think—specifically, in this case, how you think about your personal finances. Your finances are not in a black box off to the side of your life. Your finances are interwoven through every aspect of your life. Finances are intimately connected to your emotions, your past and your physical and your mental health. Just as finances impact every part of your life, conversely, there is no part of your life that does not impact your finances.

If you've had a sketchy past managing your money, independent of your childhood experiences, understand most people do. We all have memories of our own money management mistakes that were so unpleasant, we still remember them vividly years later. Money has this kind of lasting impact on our psyches and embeds itself into our emotions. Your responses to your current life challenges, including financial ones, are also influenced by your emotions. Your past history impacts your current behaviors, your habits and how you will handle your future challenges, like handling money with a busy and stressful life.

Living in a money disaster is super traumatic! Additionally, there are those who have more than adequate funds for their needs, yet they are still unable to stop worrying about money. It is not surprising, therefore, that most people in America list money as their number-one stressor in life.[2] I think everyone can agree that our lives would be better if we did not have to worry so much about money. Just imagine how much more energy and enjoyment you could get from life if you did not have to worry about paying your bills each month. I want to help you get to a place where you can concentrate on your life rather than always ruminating over your finances (or the other side of the coin where you avoid thinking about your finances at all costs). I want you to be at a place in your life where money is not one of your top stressors.

Gaining clarity concerning your money is a vital gateway to happiness and serenity. We all know that money can't buy happiness, but it will provide us with the freedom that allows us to seek happiness on our own terms.[3] Human beings also have an overwhelming need to feel they are in control of their lives, which is critical to maintaining good mental health and resilience. Various studies have shown time and time again that life satisfaction is rated higher when a feeling of control over our lives is accompanied by adequate financial resources.[4]

Now that we have clearly defined our goal (going from a money disaster and chaos to financial prosperity and serenity) and our most prominent roadblock (our subconscious beliefs that lead to subconscious thoughts and then to sabotaging behaviors), how are we going to get to prosperity? That's the burning question I have been trying to answer since 2008.

The traditional/historical view to creating prosperity is that if I provide you great personal financial educational to improve your financial literacy, it will improve your money management habits. As a long-time financial educator, my heart longs for this simple and elegant solution to the problem of improving my students' financial lives. Unfortunately, I know all too well that financial education or financial literacy training is rarely enough to improve daily financial habits—or even reduce or stop destructive ones. The current literature and research into financial literacy backs up my observations that financial education will not typically change a student's money habits.[5] Therefore, we can conclude:

Financial Education ≠ Prosperity

> *Money is never just about math! Your feelings, likely generated from your past experiences, rudely push their way into your money management efforts and sabotage them.*

For example, take the man who habitually refuses to spend any money at all. He has plenty of money but refuses to part with it. He will not spend money, even on essential bills he knows he must pay, for fear of losing control of what he has. He knows full well his behavior cannot be sustained. Yet, he persists in his attempts to hoard his money. Obviously, much more is going on there than simple math or managing a personal budget. This brings us back to our attempts to solve the formula and create the prosperity we desire.

Another recent attempt to improve financial education and overcome the behavioral roadblocks to our prosperity proposed that students might triumph over their self-defeating beliefs and habits if financial education was presented within a goal-setting paradigm. Goal setting is an extremely successful, well-known change agent that can help the student behave differently with their personal finances in the future.

The financial training literature suggested the best method to create change in students' financial habits is to make sure they emotionally connect with their financial goals during the education/ training.[6] Students must really desire the lifestyle and benefits of their new goals. I tried this technique in many classes. I emphasized that you can create prosperity if you emotionally connect with your financial goals—which is an attempt to use your feelings to assist you in changing your financial behaviors and daily habits. I spent considerable classroom time talking about goal setting and how achieving goals would create a better life for the students. In my smaller classes, I had students explain to me what achieving their goal(s) would mean to them. I found that this method did work better, but only slightly. So now, we have the following summary equation:

$$\text{Financial Education} + \text{Goal Setting} \neq \text{Prosperity}$$

This approach remains substandard, and with a few minor exceptions, does not create routine financial behavior improvements. Emphasizing goal setting produced a small group of students who left the classroom and went about the hard work of changing their actual financial behaviors. Most students in my financial classes remained psychologically resistant to behavioral change even if they thought they wanted to make a change during our classroom time together.

So why can't—or won't—most people change their financial behaviors, even when they are emotionally connected to financial goals they value and provided with the information they need to achieve those goals?

This book offers the well-researched and proven propo-
sition that poor money management is usually a symptom
of much larger life problems interfering with the students'
efforts to gain control of their financial lives. Money
management, in and of itself, is rarely the primary issue
plaguing most peoples' money problems.

If a person has persistent money issues, it is typically a symptom of additional, more serious problems going on in their lives.[7] It all begins with our childhood experiences. I know that some people feel that relating childhood experiences to our current problems is an overused bromide. I totally get why they feel that way, but I do not intend my comments to be taken within this context. Stay with me, and you will see how this concept makes perfect sense, is rooted firmly in science and is consistent with your own beliefs and knowledge.

Rather than the term childhood traumatic experiences (that I used earlier), psychologists now use what they feel is a more accurate term, "adverse childhood experiences." The foundation of our understanding in this area is based on the findings of the groundbreaking Adverse Childhood Experiences Study (ACE Study).

The ACE study shows a child perceives certain events in their childhood as averse to his or her survival. Examples of such events include child neglect, sexual victimization and child abuse; however, adverse childhood experiences need not be that severe to create lasting consequences.

The theory is that these adverse experiences are highly correlated (related to) with later destructive lifestyle choices, including smoking, overeating, under-eating, drinking and drug use. ACE also shows a very strong correlation between adverse childhood experiences and later adult negative health conditions like higher stress levels, lower fitness levels, various preventable health problems, lower social support and even a shorter life expectancy.[8]

> The harm of adverse childhood experiences upon our future does not stop there. What might surprise you is that ACE has also been strongly correlated in at least one study with dysfunctional, personal money management practices as well.[9] So there is a strong connection between ACE, defective money stories, and accompanying self-defeating behaviors.

Luckily, a person's adverse childhood experiences can be offset by protective and resilience factors. For example, having someone who loves you or cares about you in your life or belonging to a group that honors your opinion or contributions are protective factors. These protective factors can offset high ACE scores.

What are the self-defeating financial behaviors that are highly correlated with adverse childhood experiences? Michelle Bohls, couples' counselor and an expert in helping clients and couples overcome financial issues, states that most financial self-defeating financial behaviors can be grouped into four broad categories:

1. Overspending or debting
2. Underspending or financial neglect of our needs
3. Under earning or underemployment
4. Lying to ourselves and others about our finances[10]

The first self-defeating behavior, overspending or debting, is creating large debt and the interest owed from these debts. Purchasing items, even on credit, provides feelings of excitement and anticipation that most people really enjoy. It gives the buyers a break from their daily stress and anxiety that we all constantly face daily. Unfortunately, regret is the second (stronger) feeling that quickly follows feeling of "purchasing joy." We label this self-defeating cycle (spending and then regretting) as the "relief of spending" as a shorthand because it is such a common theorem throughout this book.[11]

Another common reason for debting behavior is subconsciously pretending to yourself and others that you have more money than you do. In this book, we will refer to people who like to represent themselves as being much wealthier than they actually are as "pretenders." Pretenders use debt to purchase big-ticket consumer items, such as cars or large houses, to give the impression they have much more money than they actually do. It's a very common behavior in our society. These people desire to create the impression to the outside world as being successful, competent, and upwardly mobile. The problem is, they are self-sabotaging themselves with significant debt. This is one of several reasons people who make a lot of money end up broke!

I am actually guilty of "pretending!" I must constantly monitor my own desires, wants and needs to weed this behavior out. Otherwise, I would drive new, expensive sports cars or pickup trucks all the time. I made the decision long ago to pass on new cars because I'd much rather travel all over the world instead.

The second self-defeating behavior is underspending or financial neglect. This typically involves refusing to spend money on the things you require, such as medicine, doctor appointments, dentist appointments or even paying bills that are due. This causes misery, serious self-neglect and creates an array of personal and relationship problems. The under-spender links how much money they have to their physical survival.[12] The more money they have, the safer they feel.

The third self-defeating behavior is under-earning or under-employment. This is where people stay in a job that does not pay an amount equal to their contributions, or they are underpaid compared to others in similar jobs. Some are too anxious and depressed to properly negotiate a competitive salary or to hustle for more business. There are also cases where those who are able to work do not work up to their full potential to make more money or they are unwilling to work the hours they need to pay their expenses. Of course, these people are also unwilling to make sacrifices to live within their financial means—hence the problem. Common self-defeating behavior in this category includes individuals refusing to seek treatment for associated anxiety and depression. It's not that they can't afford the treatment. They simply don't want to do it.

Lying to ourselves and others is the last broad category of self-defeating behaviors. We tell ourselves stories to justify our spending when we absolutely know better than to make certain purchases. Financial infidelity is where you lie to your partner about your spending and purchases, which destroys trust and splits couples apart all the time. In the worst cases, offenders hide secret bank accounts or loans from their spouses. These behaviors stem from feelings of shame, feelings of failure, a lack of clarity about where the money is going and from hiding information to avoid the associated negative feelings that are the primary drivers of self-defeating behavior.[13]

At this point, we've discussed several concepts and behaviors that factor into self-defeating financial decisions, so let's bring all these concepts together to show how they work in unison to hurt or help you. Do you think people who struggle with self-defeating financial decisions understand they need to make changes? Of course they do! Unfortunately, change rarely occurs or occurs at an unsatisfactory level. Despite several attempts, they just can't stop themselves. So why does this problem persist even when these individuals want to change?

Michelle Bohls and I submit that there are forces at work (typically from adverse childhood experiences) that create internal, irrational beliefs in spenders' unconscious minds. Take the example: "I am powerless or I don't deserve good things in life." Subconscious, irrational beliefs from our past create painful emotions in us. Spenders engage in self-defeating behaviors— spending or debting—to reduce stress and help them avoid the feelings and emotions flowing from their unconscious, internal programing.

Resolving to spend less does nothing to work out those internal forces that created the spending in the first place. After all, how many times have you personally vowed to spend less and not actually done it? I know I have many times! If we don't acknowledge our negative feelings and our irrational beliefs, we create persistent (unconscious) thoughts and dysfunctional behaviors. When we push our feelings away, we end up making poor choices and repeatedly performing self-defeating behaviors to avoid negative and painful thoughts and emotions. Poor choices (like creating debt or not opening your mail to avoid your bills) reinforces irrational, unconscious beliefs and increases the emotions that flow from our subconscious.

However, if we can acknowledge our beliefs and negative feelings, we are one step closer to creating prosperity in our lives. This allows us the freedom to make tough choices, like controlling our spending or choosing what we spend our money on. Once we are successful at implementing some goal-directed behaviors, it begins to disprove our negative internal beliefs to our unconscious mind and begins to improve our unconscious self-esteem.

With this new information, we can now integrate this concept into our formula. We first deal with the unconscious emotions stemming from our past adverse childhood experiences, add the life-changing power of goal setting and then add the knowledge gained from a financial education to create a new formula that will allow us to create financial success.

Eliminating Self-defeating Behaviors + Goal Setting + Financial Education = Prosperity and Serenity

I call this formula the Breakthrough Formula for Financial Prosperity! The breakthrough approach is designed to solve a very important goal for American society. That goal is to help you, and the millions of people just like you, who are living in a money disaster to progress through personal challenges and create a new life of prosperity and serenity.

The Breakthrough Formula is different from normal approaches, and it is more effective because it starts from the premise that your finances are not a stand-alone item but are interrelated to every single aspect of your life. Your finances are related to your emotional health, your unconscious beliefs, and your physical health. As strange as it might seem, everyone's finances are irrevocably linked to their past.

Conversely, if you are financially fit, your life is likely going reasonably well because you are avoiding (or minimizing) an entire array of self-sabotaging behaviors that negatively impact your finances and your daily life. You have clarity around your money.

You understand how much is coming in and how much is going out. You know exactly how much money you have! You feel good about the choices you have, even if there are only a few. Most of all, you don't have shame surrounding your money usage.

Each and every element of the breakthrough equation is vitally important. If I take any one of the elements away, then the equation will no longer work. For example, if I take away financial education, one cannot effectively utilize goal-based behaviors without knowing what to do and when to do it. Yet, financial education alone can't get you there. Without goal setting, you really don't understand where you are headed, so little improvement can occur. If you don't deal with your self-defeating behaviors, you will repeatedly sabotage your own financial and life improvement efforts. Based on current research, our personal experience and the data provided in this text, these three elements in our breakthrough equation represent your best chance of transforming your current money disaster to a life of prosperity and serenity.

The Breakthrough Formula for Prosperity shows us the way to move past all the many roadblocks we will encounter on our journey to financial abundance. We always begin by eliminating or reducing the harm caused by our internal, subconscious money lessons we learned from our past and the accompanying life problems those lessons created for us. We then educate ourselves about our goal and how to move forward. Finally, we set goals to overcome the inevitable roadblocks that hinder our progress.

We have covered a lot of negative topics so far, so here's some good news: you are not the only person in this boat. In fact, you have to stand in line to get on board! Many people in your life and periphery struggle with the challenges you are facing right now. It is very easy to feel that you are all alone with your problems, but I can confidently say that most everyone has some form of shame connected to money—having too much money, not having enough money or how we use our money. Someone making a lot of money can have as much shame as someone making almost none.

We like to hide our money shame from others and try our best to ignore it. All of the 12-step programs include a section about shame and silence. We are only as sick as our secrets! Your silence only reinforces your shame. Breaking the silence and talking about these issues will reduce your shame and the negative energy surrounding it.

Now here is some even better news: many people who faced similar money problems have gone from living in a money disaster to creating a life filled with prosperity. They have increased their financial standing and their subsequent life satisfaction. I will demonstrate beyond almost any reasonable doubt that it can be done. To further illustrate this point, I've included as many stories as I can recall in this book about average people who overcame their own serious financial issues and problems. *See the workbook section for each chapter for inspirational stories about people who conquered these life problems and achieved financial prosperity.*

Now for the best news of all: you can begin to understand and recognize your own emotions stemming from your own unconscious, illogical beliefs. Once you have a better understanding of and release those trapped feelings, it will be a big step forward to overcoming the unconscious self-defeating behaviors that are sabotaging you. You also have the power to modify the lessons you learned from your past experiences in your mind. Then, you can utilize goal-directed behaviors to overcome the roadblocks you face. That, combined with some financial knowledge, gives you a great shot at creating prosperity and peace. Increased financial success through implementing goal-based behaviors will also increase your self-esteem, feelings of self-worth and self-efficacy, which is the confidence that you can do it and are in control of your own life.[14]

Are you finally ready to look at the illogical beliefs and negative emotions that are derailing your financial behaviors? Are you ready to see if that is what is causing your unconscious, self-defeating behaviors? Why not challenge yourself to start by shifting just one behavior? It could make a huge difference in your life!

This book can help guide you by providing you with the following information:

1. How your money issues are related to your self-defeating beliefs and behaviors
2. Financial education tailored to your unique situation(s)
3. Motivation to apply our breakthrough formula to your life and finances
4. Tips and strategies on managing your self-defeating behaviors so you can succeed
5. How to create a life with a purpose that will bring you happiness, meaning and, ultimately, prosperity

Chapter 1 Summary Formulas

The Breakthrough Formula For Prosperity

Financial Education + Goal Setting +
Eliminating Self-Defeating Behaviors
= Prosperity & Serenity

THE BREAKTHROUGH FORMULA FOR FINANCIAL PROSPERITY.

SERENTIY & PROSPERITY

ELIMINATING SELF DEFEATING BELIEFS & BEHAVIORS

GOAL SETTING

FINANCIAL EDUCATION

Chapter 2
From Money Disaster to Success Story

How would you complete the below sentence?

_____ is the biggest factor keeping me from being happy right now.

> Money experiences or stories from your past can cause
> you to repeat the same money mistakes over and over
> again in an endless loop. To free yourself from your
> past, you must break free from this loop.

S tudents in my financial literacy classes all have their own unique money histories from which spring unique money problems. They come to my class knowing full well they have some financial aspects of their life that are dysfunctional. During all of my many classes, only a handful of people have ever been willing to say in a public setting, "I am terrible with money," "I am always having money problems" or even, "I am having this specific life issue that is negatively impacting my finances." Those that do speak up in class are very brave, and I always congratulate them for showing courage.

Most people who have any kind of money issues typically have deep shame surrounding their money performance and simply will not discuss their real money problems. They sit there quietly and say nothing as we discuss money management, and all the while, their insides are churning, and they feel shame they are too terrified to openly express. Sadly, the person they are sitting next to likely has a similar problem. Sitting silently mutually reinforces each persons' silence and shame.

The most common money story involves the stress of meeting our monthly financial obligations, the shame of falling short of the money expectations we set for ourselves and the anxiety and worry that comes from not having any idea how to fix our financial problems. This leaves us feeling "money stupid," inadequate and very ashamed of our money performance.[1]

You may even feel deep shame since you knew full well you were making a mistake when you took a particular action or made a past purchase. Yet, you went ahead and did it anyway. As a result, you may become very angry with yourself. I know I have done this several times. When we do something that we perceive as negative, we naturally internalize our feelings and blow this up in our minds as, "I am bad!" The subsequent series of reactions and feelings are interpreted by your mind and body as shame. In short, shame stems from failing to forgive yourself for your mistakes and the anger you feel toward yourself. As you can see from the shame example above, it is an undeniable fact that we are very emotionally connected to our concept of money, and this concept is directly linked to our self-image.

I believe this is the real reason our parents' culture never wanted to discuss money—not necessarily because it was "private" but because they knew full well they had made terrible mistakes along the way and were embarrassed and angry with themselves for making those mistakes. They had money shame. One of the characteristics of shame is that it causes people to keep secrets from everyone—even from their families.

Of course, shame is not the only feeling we get when we think of finances. Our deep emotional connection with money was formed through the early family socialization process and was coined your "money script," as explained by Brad Klontz Psy.D. and Ted Klontz, Ph.D. in their famous book, *Mind Over Money.*[2] Their book describes how we form attitudes, opinions, unconscious beliefs and emotions surrounding the way we manage money. The Klontzes were the pioneers in the field of behavioral finance, and they were among the first to describe why our financial behaviors with money can be both dysfunctional and unhelpful.

The Klontzs' theory is that your money script is the story you learned about money as a child and the subsequent emotional impact it had upon you while growing up.

> *Your money experiences are infused with the beliefs and emotions your parents exhibited about money during your childhood. These beliefs and emotions were rarely stated out loud but were continually demonstrated by your parents and/or caregivers. Money dysfunction is widely spread throughout the general population and is found in all socioeconomic positions in society.*[3]

The money script we inherit from our families can be likened to a witch's curse. As an analogy, an evil witch, offended by some slight, attached a curse to your great-great-grandfather to make him dysfunctional with money. Now, this curse is passed down from parent to child down through your family's generations.

Your money script or money story plays out entirely within your subconscious. Your story creates unconscious belief(s) that are very powerful because they are hard to examine and challenge. They don't come to the surface often, and you only get glimpses of them on rare occasions.

A common analogy is that your beliefs are like a computer operating system. The operating system runs entirely in the background without your knowledge. Most people run the programs or applications they need but know very little about the actual computer operating system's rules. Your money script is similar. It is always running in your subconscious and provides you with the structure and rules that you typically operate within. All too often, these subconscious beliefs create poor financial outcomes and unhappiness for us. Continuing the analogy, our software won't run as well if our operating system has a logic flaw. In addition, these unconscious beliefs are anchored in emotions. Emotional beliefs are more powerful than any facts we know. It is this emotional connection that gives our unconscious money scripts power over our behaviors.

We briefly mentioned some of these unconscious, self-limiting beliefs in Chapter 1. In this chapter, we'll get more detailed and also cover how limiting beliefs can also be learned and absorbed from other sources. You can get negative beliefs about money from your church, "Rich people can't go to heaven." Or, you might get these beliefs from your extended family, such as a shared hatred of the rich. Some of these limiting beliefs might even be gender messages from outdated, sexist cultural beliefs, such as women aren't good with math, women spend too much money shopping, men are supposed to be the breadwinners or men have no idea what the household expenses are.

Without even realizing it, you watched and participated in your own unique money story growing up in your family dynamic. Think back to your childhood and the unspoken lessons might be clearer. Those stories provided you with the subliminal messages, subsequent beliefs, and the emotions that your subconscious brain now believes to be accurate and true—whether they are valid or not. You unconsciously believe these money stories down to your innermost core because you lived them! These thoughts create dysfunctional actions that you will repeat endlessly unless you challenge and change them.

Examples of defective money stories and their explanations:

- Only greedy people have money. (I don't want to be greedy, so I can't have money.)
- Money is too difficult to manage, so why even try? (I can't get rich through hard work or by being a good person.)
- Only rich people get ahead. Everyone else is poor. (The rich are evil and take advantage of others, so I don't want to be seen as being rich.)
- The system is rigged against you. (I can't get ahead no matter what I do because the rich rigged the economic system against me, and hard work won't help me.)
- The rich stole all their money from poor people. (I don't want to be seen as a thief, so I can never be rich.)
- Spend all your money now because you won't have it tomorrow. (Everyone must spend their money as soon as they get it.)

- I need a partner to help me manage money. (I am not enough and/or I am not worthy of wealth.)
- I dislike poor people, so I have to save every penny so I never become poor. (If I spend money, I could become poor, or my spending could get out of control.)
- If I spend money on something I need, want and can afford, I may never be able to stop spending money. (If I spend money on myself, I will be just like my parent who always spent all our money and kept us poor.)

Consider the example, "Money is too difficult to control, so why even try?" One would likely think, "That is simply a ridiculous thought!" Yet, this is the money story many of us unconsciously absorbed from our past. This story now seeks to control many of our actions unless we actively try to change our unconscious thoughts.

We all initially live out the money script we inherited from our family and society. If your childhood was very dysfunctional, your money script is likely built upon a defective foundation. Or your money script might be impacted by your own feelings of low self-worth stemming from a less-than-ideal upbringing. The defective foundation creates the genesis of your dysfunctional, repeating money behaviors.

When we first leave the nest, we continue to live the money script that we were taught as children, so the "witch's curse" continues through us via our beliefs and subsequent actions based on those beliefs. Growing up in a dysfunctional money environment (as many of us did) increases your chances of also being bad with money. This is how the curse is able to live on and is passed down through the generations.[4]

Later, we each create our own unique money script that is separate from that of our immediate family. Unfortunately, many times our own money script is also a maladjusted ball of rolling incompetence. So the money dysfunction curse (stemming from a lack of knowledge and faulty money stories that are rooted in past family dysfunction) is passed down from us to our offspring and so on.

Do you ever have the thought, "Money always goes wrong for me! Why do I have so many money problems? I have terrible luck!" Others have these same types of thoughts and emotions stemming from their past dysfunctional families' money stories. Maybe we were told by our parents or caregivers that we were stupid, or we were criticized often and given the impression that we were inadequate. These thoughts and childhood experiences can derail us today. If you have these feelings and the accompanying shame, you are not very likely to want to talk to anyone about these feelings.

> Dysfunctional false childhood messages are insidiously evil and appear to be self-fulfilling prophecies. For example, if you believe subconsciously that you are bad with money and you then make a money mistake, like borrowing money at too high an interest rate, then you believe you have just proven all your self-criticisms to be accurate and true! This a very powerful thought loop, even if it is entirely a false one.

This thought loop will likely drive future dysfunctional money behaviors in the future. After all, you just proved to yourself that you are terrible with money, rather than the alternative theory, which is that everyone makes money mistakes once in a while. You ignore all the counter information that proves that you are really smart, while focusing in on the self-fulfilling expectations that you are bad with your money.

Our feelings about money and how it can impact us can be explained this way: we never entirely escape our family or our past.[5] Also, chronic self-defeating financial behaviors are rarely driven by conscious or rational thought.[6] You may know exactly what to do in most money situations, but for some unknown reason you never do it! So begins your money story's repeating loop that is part and parcel of the witch's curse.

When you make a concerted effort to correct your repeating mistake, it is common to jump to a polar opposite problematic behavior. For example, an extreme spender might then turn into an extreme saver. Or you might jump between these two extremes repeatedly.[7] This behavior is believed to be caused by the internal self-belief that you just don't deserve to be happy! The internal dialogue, "I don't deserve to be happy" creates emotions that influence subsequent actions and create misery in your life through miserly underspending or self-neglect in order to avoid being happy and proving your inner self-defeating beliefs. These behaviors may involve skimping on healthy foods or not seeing a doctor when you need to—which likely makes you very unhappy and miserable. When you try to correct your miserly behavior, your belief about not deserving to be happy is still present. Because you still don't deserve to be happy, you begin creating new misery for yourself by overspending and running up your debt.

The same person has a consistent belief system, "I don't deserve to be happy." The emotion the person feels from this belief remains exactly the same. However, the emotions fuel two entirely separate self-defeating behaviors, but the person still creates misery in both behaviors by feeling they don't have the right to be happy. When underspending is forbidden, the subconscious just uses a different technique to prevent you from obtaining happiness. The subconscious fuels the next behavior (overspending) to accomplish that goal. This pattern continues in an endless loop of both self- and financial sabotage.

How can we break this loop? We can use the Breakthrough Formula for Prosperity and change our destructive money behaviors by first changing our beliefs, changing our scripts, and modifying the lessons we learned during our money socialization period. We can feel and then release our emotions rooted in our past experiences that are holding us back in the present. With just a little work, your future can be very different from your past. This is how we begin to break our dysfunctional looping behaviors.

Change your destructive subconscious money thoughts and behaviors by implementing these three steps:

1. Determine what messages you received from your family and environment. *(See workbook section to help identify your own childhood money story.)*
2. Forgive yourself for past mistakes.
3. Reframe your past into a more positive story.

The first step is to figure out what messages you received from your childhood in relation to money management. Once you have a better understanding of the messages you are subliminally playing on a looping soundtrack in your head, you can alter your money thought loop to create more positive and productive behaviors.

There are two types of messages; the first is subliminal, or messages that were never spoken. These are the lessons you learned observing your parents and by participating in your family unit growing up. The second type of message we learn as children are the ones that were repeatedly stated outright. Many of us were told, "You are bad," or "You are worthless!" or the worst, "Why are you so stupid?"

> Once we understand that these negative messages and self-views were taught and they are not some immutable law of nature assigned to us in particular, it is much easier to unlearn this faulty messaging. After beginning to unlearn these messages, we can create better, more productive thoughts and accompanying behaviors.

The second step is to forgive yourself. Understand you did the best you could with the situation and knowledge you had.

> Say this aloud, "I forgive myself for my mistakes." Say it several times a day for a while until it becomes your automatic thought whenever you think of some past money failure.

Whenever I recall moments that cause me shame from my past behavior, I have trained myself to say mentally, "I have forgiven myself for this mistake." In a perfect world, you would have learned what you needed to know when you were young and avoided such mistakes (also, your family life would have been supportive and positive). It is not a perfect world, so we now must find the way to move forward to a more positive future. It is up to you now to make sure you forgive yourself for your mistakes. Forgiving yourself is priority.

The third step is to understand that the memories of your past held in your brain are not fixed, but are surprisingly flexible and change over time. You create these memories anew whenever you recall a previous event. Contrary to popular belief, they are not stored in a file cabinet and taken out when you want to remember a past event. Each memory must be created again in your brain each time you recall it. This constant construction makes your memories extremely vulnerable to change.

For example, witnesses give inaccurate information about past events all the time. They are not lying; they honestly believe the things they remember. Having a flexible memory is why the police are careful to separate witnesses in a criminal event. Hearing someone else's story about an event you just witnessed will likely influence or outright change how you remember an event—a very troublesome fact for police officers—but very useful to us and for our purposes here.

You can apply this lesson to your unique money script. For example, if you were taught that only greedy, rich people hoard money, this subliminal message and its accompanying emotions might cause you to never save money. If you never save any money, then you cannot possibly become rich and become one of these "greedy" people.[8]

If you reframed that memory by redefining greedy as "taking more than is fair or needed" then you can reframe this concept. Your reframe could then be, "I trust myself to take only what is fair and give the excess to those who inspire me—or those who are in need."

There can also be a very positive progression in your reframe. As an example, you could reframe your past experiences from "I do stupid things with my money" to "Past financial mistakes taught me important lessons and provide me with the motivation I need to succeed and overcome future financial obstacles." You could then progress to the thought, "My difficult past molded me into a person who wants to succeed!" The next progression you could work on is, "I am driven to succeed!" The great thing about these reframes are they can be absolutely true!

> *Reframing our memories and giving them a new context is the method we use to modify our unhealthy money scripts that prevent us from obtaining financial freedom and serenity. Defective money scripts, beliefs and their accompanying behaviors can easily become self-fulfilling mind loops or traps. Reframing allows us to escape our circular and dysfunctional thinking.*

Your negative inner script is a false premise that is based only on a few misinterpreted data points from your past and needs to be rethought and replaced. Society does its share of sabotaging your money story as well with common stereotypes. This way of thinking is inaccurate and should be rejected and replaced by improved thinking and clarity.

The Breakthrough Formula for Prosperity has an education element to create the needed thought change. You might read biographies about great leaders, such as Ursula Burns who is a top corporate leader and the past CEO of Xerox. Or, if you were told you were stupid growing up (or felt stupid) then read biographies about people like Stephen King who failed miserably at first but kept trying and succeeded. *Read more inspiring stories in the work-book section.*

As I mentioned earlier, I received the message as a young person that I was stupid and lazy. I have learned, through re-framing my own story, that what I was taught was not real! My reframe is that my experiences had to do with my mother and father's emotional issues much more than it ever had to do with me. The money story I was taught about myself has now been proven to have been entirely wrong. I have unequivocally shown that I am not lazy and I am actually great with my money.

This chapter has shown that our past can hold us back from future financial success by creating unconscious, untrue beliefs and accompanying behaviors to make those beliefs come true. As you like-ly already suspect, every negative internal belief stemming from your past experiences impacts not only your money management success but many other aspects of your life as well. If your inner/subconscious belief is, "I am not good enough and I don't deserve good things in life," you can bet the farm this belief will also sabotage other aspects of your life besides money management—like your relationship with your partner for example. This is another reason these defective money stories or scripts can be so harmful to our lives.

As you recall, there is a lot more to the Breakthrough Formula for Financial Prosperity than just managing your money and life problems. For instance, how would you like to create your own version of a perfect life? How about a life that thrills you and gives you the best chance to find happiness and inner serenity entirely on your terms? Then you certainly want to add goal setting to your life. Goals provide us with greater purpose and direction, define our values, improve our self-confidence, and increase our life suc-cess exponentially. Learn how to create financial prosperity with goals in the next chapter.

Chapter 2 Summary Formulas

What You Learned About Money as a Child +
Emotional Impact = Money Script or Story

Dysfunction + Unhelpful Money Emotions =
Defective Money Script or Story

Emotions About Money Passed on to Your
Offspring = Money Script

Shame + Anxiety + Avoidance
= Money Dysfunction

Chapter 3
From Financial Mishap to Goals of Abundance

How would you complete the below sentences?

I would like my life's greatest accomplishment to be
_____.

If I accomplished _____, I would have
more control over my life.

Becoming a millionaire was always my goal from the moment I began setting goals as a confused and troubled teen. When I began my job at the police department, I was saving $50 a month in my investment accounts ($25 in each bi-weekly paycheck). I kept working on increasing my savings and putting that money into my investment accounts.

My road to wealth was never a smooth one. As all people who accomplish difficult goals, I was forced to overcome significant problems and roadblocks on my million-dollar quest. For example, I suffered a pretty significant bout of depression. Also, I had not one, but two divorces to overcome, along with the pain and financial problems that flows from those breakups. Divorces weren't the only bumps on my road. Years later, I lost close to $150,000 in the stock market in my investment accounts during the tech crash. I blame this loss on my own lack of knowledge and lack of understanding of how investing, diversity and market cycles work together. Also, there was a time I ran my savings numbers through various charts (apps weren't available then) and determined I was not saving nearly enough from the monthly budget to achieve my goal. I had to radically change what I was doing to increase the amount I was saving to make this goal workable. But together, my wife and I crushed this goal and so many others!

Achieving this goal was everything I hoped it would be and more. As a result, my wife and I now get to travel all over the world. We can go on adventures for a month or more at a time. When not traveling, the activity we most enjoy, we can come and go as we please. It allows me the freedom to write and follow my dreams, while allowing her to pick and choose what she will or will not do. We answer to no one but each other. This is truly the life we envisioned and designed for ourselves from the ground up. Since becoming financially independent, we have lived in three different states to be closer to our family. We might or might not live in three more before we are done.

The Breakthrough Formula for Prosperity relies upon goal setting as an essential element in the journey from financial disaster to prosperity. Goal setting is so important in this formula because it provides you with a positive view of your future and takes you to places you want to be, rather than aimlessly walking through life and arriving at some random destinations. It gives our life meaning, context and even purpose. It provides each of us with the conditions that give us our best shot at happiness, assuming we have aligned our life with our goals and values. Finally, accomplishing goals increases our self-confidence and self-esteem. Goal accomplishment is one of the most important things you can do with your life. It is literally what makes our most precious dreams come true.

So how did I overcome the many life and financial problems that held me back? Well, through more goal setting, of course! Even though I encountered difficulties, as does everyone who reaches for their dreams, I kept persevering. I refocused and modified my goals to overcome any problem I was facing, continually revised my plans, and always moved forward. I will admit that I did wonder several times if I could actually make it. In fact, I had several friends who actually told me bluntly I would never make it. Luckily, I didn't believe them. Now, my newest goal is to create two million. Hey, the first million is always the hardest!

Goal setting can improve every aspect of your life. You can set goals for anything in life, from relationships to professional accomplishments. Here is a partial list of the goals I set and achieved.

· Graduate-level education with no school debt
· Professional accomplishments far beyond my initial imagining
· Finding a partner who shares my values, goals, and vision of the future
· Domestic harmony, or as much domestic harmony as two people can have
· Overcoming PTSD-related symptoms and behaviors
· Create life conditions that provide me with my best shot at happiness
· Obtain the freedom to do exactly what I want to do today and tomorrow
· Traveled all over the world
· Create a life purpose that fulfills me

I detailed this journey in my award-winning book, *Messages from Your Future: The Seven Rules for Financial, Personal, and Professional Success.*[1] I explained how setting goals activates our minds and the substantial powers that exist in our universe to accomplish the things we set our sights and minds upon. Goals combined with directed effort can create an unbeatable inertia that powers us into a future we choose rather than the one we happen upon. There is no better way to improve your life in a self-directed way. You begin by envisioning your ideal life, and then set goals that will bring your vision to reality.

Your journey to accomplishing important goals consistent with your values begins with fully understanding and accepting the Ironclad Rule of Accountability:

> *The Ironclad Rule of Accountability states that you and you alone are responsible for most outcomes you obtain or fail to obtain in life.*[2]

To overcome various life problems and utilize the Breakthrough Formula for Financial Prosperity to its maximum effectiveness you must now assume total responsibility for what you do about the unfortunate things that happened to you in life. The only important consideration to life's many mishaps—and there will be many—is what are you going to do about said problem(s) now? In some instances, you are the one who made the mistake that produced your crappy situation. Every human being has made some reasonably serious errors in their life and this is particularly true when it comes to finances.

However, the time has come to do something radically different. Leave your self-blame, shame, and any regrets behind you. All of your mistakes are just old news, so don't dwell on them. Forgive yourself, take the knowledge you gained from your mistakes, leave everything else, then move on. You will have a lot of work to do, and you can't carry the heavy weight of regrets, self-blame, and shame around with you. Now, shift your focus to setting goals with the purpose of making the changes you desire to feel better emotionally, financially, and spiritually. Go create the positive life outcomes you need for your best life and your happiness!

I can tell you from hard-won experience, goal setting provides mental structure and helps you harness the powers of our universe to create what you most want and desire in life. You can manifest both material and intangible outcomes almost out of thin air! This does not, however, alleviate you doing your part. You perform the direct actions needed to make things happen. Wanting something is only the first step. Taking action is the essential second step.

To be effective, goals must meet six specific requirements:

1. You must believe deep down in your heart that you can do it.
2. You must deeply desire the benefits of the goal(s).
3. You must set goals that are specific and measurable (time, date, place, plan, etc.).
4. Goals should be written.
5. Make your goals part of your identity.
6. Take positive actions that are goal-based.

You must be convinced that you are able to accomplish the goal you envisioned. Believe it, say it, and leave no room for mental doubt. Know that you can do it with your entire being. If you don't believe something is possible, then you certainly can't accomplish it. Humans first create the world they live in mentally with their beliefs, and then they physically inhabit the world they've created with their minds.

Take the example of Roger Bannister. He ran the first sub-four-minute mile. Before his achievement in 1954, it was thought human beings might not be able to run that fast.[3] But he believed he could, so he trained hard. His belief and accompanying work toward this goal enabled him to be the first person to run a mile in under four minutes. After he did it, many others were able to as well because the mental barriers of what humans were capable of fell away.

Consider the naysayers who told me that I could not possibly create wealth by saving and investing my wages as a cop. "No! It is not possible," they said. In fact, the comment I often got was, "You can't get rich doing this job!" They didn't believe they could do it, so naturally they projected their doubts about their own abilities onto me. Maybe they were right about themselves, but they were absolutely wrong about me. The primary difference was I believed that I could do it, and I did.

Think about prisoners who successfully rebuild their lives and finances after being released from jail. They truly believed they could change their lives and they desired the benefits of the goals they set. Setting goals you truly desire that are in line with your values automatically causes your brain to evaluate the steps needed to achieve your goal and prioritize your actions to create the outcomes you want.[4] This requires visualizing the amazing benefits your goal will provide to you. That visualization will be what you hold onto when the going gets tough.

Your goals must also be specific and measurable and not general thoughts or daydreams. For example, "I want to be wealthy in the future" is not nearly as effective as, "I want to have a net worth of 1.5 million dollars in 20 years on (specific date)." Specifics give you a measurable bar to weigh your efforts and progress against. Specific, measurable goals take some time to evolve in your mind because they require detailed thought.

So, write your goals down. This is a step many people like to skip. Don't! Writing your goals down fully activates your brain, your intentions and creates the desire in your mind to develop an efficient path to success. A good example of the importance of writing goals can be found in the book, *Goals! How to Get Everything You Want—Faster Than You Ever Thought Possible,* by Brian Tracy. Tracy points out that Harvard MBA graduates who took the time to write out their career and life goals (only 3% of the graduating class) earned 10 times more than their non-goal-oriented fellow graduates 10 years later.[5]

The process I have developed over time is as follows: I write a detailed plan (see planning chapter) to achieve my goal. Then I post the sheet on or near my bathroom mirror so I can see it every day. That helps me refocus and helps me hold myself accountable for achieving the steps required to turn my goal into a reality. After a while, I have seen my goal sheet so many times in this location it blends into the background, and I don't really notice it anymore. When this happens, I move it to another location in the house that I frequent. This causes it to pop back into my vision once again.

I set a goal years ago to create a million-dollar portfolio of investments. My written goal was to create this wealth by saving and investing my wages. There are many ways to create wealth, but this is the way I chose. I realized that in order for the goal to be effective, I needed to make it part of my identity. I assimilated the goal into my identity by working on some aspect of it every day. I also discussed my goal with others (accountability) and constantly researched ways to make it happen.

The last requirement for effective goals is to take action. Just sitting in your chair won't make it happen. Roger Bannister didn't break the four-minute mile by simply visualizing. He trained diligently with purpose. The process of goal achievement is known to enhance your skills and abilities as you move through the process. Success begets success and encourages you to take on new challenges and more risks to accomplish even greater goals.

Easy goals don't require much thought or energy. The most effective goals are those that are somewhat ambitious. Studies have shown ambitious goals are far more motivating and typically create higher performance—likely because of the thought, planning and effort that must go into accomplishing these objectives.[6] Note I said, "ambitious" not "impossible" goals. An ambitious goal motivates you to action much more than an impossible goal or daydream. (*See workbook, chapter 3*) If you consider the goal nearly impossible, you likely will never start working on it. If the goal is too easy, you also likely won't do it because it will be boring. You have to search for that sweet spot of excitement and challenge versus doability.

Of course, we all have to worry about our habits. Good habits propel us toward our goals, and bad habits sabotage our efforts and pull us back.

Chapter 3 Summary Formulas

Written, Specific & Measurable +
Date For Completion + Consistent Effort =
Effective Goal Setting

Greater Confidence + Enhanced Skills +
Increased Ability to Handle Problems +
More Life Satisfaction =
Goal Achievement

The Ironclad Rule of Accountability =
You Are Responsible For Most Life Outcomes

Chapter 4
From Bad Habits to Prosperous Habits

How would you complete the below sentences?

_____ is the one habit I would like to change. The one habit I would like to add to my life is _____.

When I was a police officer, I would meet my coworkers at a neighborhood bar/restaurant right after work. We referred to these get-togethers as "choir practice." We all worked a midnight shift, so we would meet early in the morning hours around 7:00 a.m. (Yes, bars are open at 7:00 a.m.!) We would grab something to eat and have a couple of beers before going home. This got to be a regular part of our routine. Although I enjoyed the socialization after work, it wasn't the best use of my time or money and was destroying my budget. Socializing exclusively with other police officers can create an entire spectrum of attitudinal and emotional problems that it is better to avoid. Additionally, it is definitely not healthy to drink most days of the week.

To create the needed change, I cut my participation to three days a week, then one day a week and then to once a month or so. Then

I cut back my attendance to once in a great while. I replaced my bad habits described above by socializing with a mix of people (not just police officers) by participating in several physical activities on my off-duty time rather than drinking beer and enduring the fallout of extra body weight and expense. Although initially it was discomforting, this change improved my day-to-day life and, ultimately, my finances.

Math is not really the focus of the Breakthrough Formula for Prosperity. Knowing a great deal about math, like calculating compound interest rates, determining your return on investments (ROI) and other complicated formulas really won't help you so much in your quest to travel from financial disaster to prosperity. You actually don't even need to know these formulas at all! Applications for your phone or computer are available for all the tasks mentioned above. What is actually very important for the Breakthrough Formula is the emphasis on evaluating your daily behaviors.

Your behaviors are your interactions with your current environment within the context of your past. Habits are the offspring of our beliefs and some of those beliefs support repeated behaviors that eventually become a routine or maybe even a ritual. It is by understanding, altering, controlling, or slightly changing our behaviors that we will discover prosperity. The key to the Breakthrough Formula is adopting certain behaviors that are supported by routine habits, while at the same time avoiding or discarding poor habits and behaviors.

We all have constructive (positive) and destructive (negative) habits that significantly impact our finances. Great money habits create success and improve both our life and our self-esteem. *(See workbook for habits that build financial health.)* On the other hand, engaging in negative money habits typically creates scarcity, stress, aggravation and sometimes even shame because our habits led to money failure.

CHILDHOOD EXPERIENCES

CONSCIOUS + UNCONSCIOUS THOUGHTS AND BELIEFS

BEHAVIORS

HABITS

OUTCOMES

Your money habits are likely heavily influenced by the money script or the money story you learned as a child. However, it is still possible to alter or eliminate specific daily habits that hold you back from success. Below are examples of financial habits that you might want to consider changing in order to improve your financial trajectory:

- No clarity about the amount of money you have coming in and where that money goes
- Failing to align your spending with your value system
- Procrastinating on your budget chores
- Socializing primarily at bars or restaurants (expensive and unhealthy)
- Regularly buying a new car
- Eating out every day
- Failing to record your spending
- Failure to price shop for items you need
- Living a lifestyle that does not allow you to save

Of course, you could fill several books with common, bad financial habits. Identifying and changing your bad habits will reduce your debt, increase your savings, and help you control your spending. It is also important to not try to change everything at once. Trying to change too much at one time will overwhelm you. Ideally, change one habit successfully. This will give you the energy and motivation to work on another and so on.

Human beings are creatures who love their habits. Our habits allow us to go into a type of automatic pilot mode. A good example of this would be driving and listening to a podcast at the same time. When you are driving to your destination while concentrating on a podcast, you may realize later you actually remember very little of the drive. The reason is you were on automatic pilot and were engaged in the routine habit of driving. The same is true of your morning or bedtime routines.

Our brains are always looking to form habits so they can put our actions on automatic pilot. Our brain likes to form habits for two reasons:

· Habits allow your brain to work less. Therefore, up to 45% of our daily behaviors are controlled by habits—almost half our day.
· The brain loves habits because a habit equals safety as far as your brain is concerned.[1]

Charles Duhigg, one of the world's experts on habits, writes in his book, *The Power of Habit,* that all habits are made up of three separate components:

1. The "cue" which triggers the brain to begin its automatic pilot loop or habit
2. The "routine" or behavior you engage in—your actual habit
3. The brain's "reward," which could be anything from a mental boost from caffeine, a sugar boost or maybe even a game token.[2]

Cues (in the above context) can be almost anything that alerts the brain to run its habit program. It can include a time of day, a situation, a location, or an emotional state like being upset or happy. The routine is the behavior you engage in.[3] The reward can be anything the brain has come to like. Take my habit of attending the meetups after work, for example. Socializing with others lit up my brain's pleasure center then elevated my mood and lowered depression symptoms. Of course, alcohol increases dopamine and relaxes your body.

Another habit I've noticed recently is the need for people to have the newest gadgets. For example, buying a new iPhone every time Apple releases one. People gladly wait in line for hours to purchase a new iPhone at over $1,000. Why do people get roped into this habit? Part of the reason is the incredible marketing campaign by Apple. The strategy is to create a huge media buzz, followed by limited availability of their newest iPhones. Limited availability and media buzz create both desire and the fear of scarcity. This is a big motivator for some. They feel they have purchased a limited and precious commodity. By purchasing this item, it makes the buyer "unique and sophisticated." After all, most people don't have one yet and may not have one for years. They can also demonstrate how tech-savvy they are to their peers and maybe they'll have more social standing with their group. Additionally, the relief of spending allows people to defer daily life stress via the "relief of spending" phenomena. Use the new iPhone example to analyze how detrimental financial habits begin:

1. Cue: News of new iPhone release and reported scarcity
2. Routine: Go wait in line and pay a large sum for the newest iPhone model.
3. Reward: Increased social status and the "relief of spending"

Habits are formed because our brains like the reward. Once a habit is formed, however, we become emotionally attached to the habit. We might even protect the habit from those who would want you to change it—like our partners. There is a sense of loss when we stop engaging in the habit. Consider habits like drinking, smoking, snacking, caffeine, and the instant gratification of spending rather than saving money. We love these habits, and our emotional brain doesn't want us to change them. We have to overcome our emotional brain with our rational brain.

Since we now understand the habit loop and our emotional attachment to our habits, we can use this information to stop our poor financial habits and create better ones. One popular and successful technique is to replace a dysfunctional habit with a new and better habit. An example would be substituting socializing with your friends at restaurants (expensive) with taking turns socializing at each friend's home (much less expensive).

Socializing at a restaurant:

1. Cue: A need to relax and reduce stress
2. Routine: Socialize with friends at a restaurant and spend money
3. Reward: Activates the brain's pleasure centers and elevates mood

Socializing at a friend's home:

1. Cue: A need to relax and reduce stress
2. Routine: Socialize with friends without spending much money (if any)
3. Reward: Activates the brain's pleasure centers and elevates mood

Replacement behaviors, or coming up with a competing habit, has been a successful way for many people to improve their poor financial outcomes.[4] In the above example of friends meeting at a friend's home instead of a restaurant, the cue and reward were kept and only the routine was changed.

Another strategy is to change a habit's reward to something similar your brain can substitute for the previous reward you enjoyed.[5] For example, substitute a sweet fruit snack for your candy snack habit. Since we don't always fully understand what our brain is actually getting from our current habit loop, experimentation with the routine and reward will be required. Or maybe you can change the routine of the habit after you get the cue.

My favorite habit-changing strategy that I have had used with great success in the past is the gradual reduction strategy. This is the technique I mentioned earlier where you gradually reduce the unwanted behavior.[6] I have stopped several bad habits using this technique.

Another strategy I have used with success is the vacation strategy. The vacation strategy involves stopping a bad habit while on vacation. A good time to change your habits is when you are away from your house and job. When on vacation, your routine is completely different. This eliminates all the cues that used to prompt you to engage in your bad habit loop.[7] You end up not missing your bad habit while on vacation very much if at all. They key is not to start the habit back up when you return, which is bit dicier.

Another way we can eliminate our daily cues is to change our entire lifestyle.[8] The point of this technique is to change our lifestyle to a healthier one. You reimagine your life from top to bottom and go about making a plan to support your changes. The problem is that most people get overwhelmed if they take on too many lifestyle changes at once, so start slowly.

It takes about the same amount of time to start a new habit as it does to break a bad habit. The minimum time required to change, stop or start a new habit is around two months or 66 days.[9] Sometimes it takes longer (potentially a year or more), depending on how ingrained the habit is into your life and the reward your brain gets from its habit. A lot of self-help gurus talk about a time period of 21 days to change a habit, but a minimum of 66 days is based on habit change research and is a more accurate representation of the minimum time needed. In the end, it will take as long as it takes to change poor habits and build better ones. Depending upon their specific habits, some people struggle with the change process for several years before they finally get the job done.

You can combine the information in this chapter and make it work to your benefit. To explain how to utilize this information, let's take a look at a theoretical lifestyle that leaves you with a zero balance in savings each month. I think this problem is pretty relatable, as most of us have been there. Let us assume each month you spend every dime that is available to you on bills and various other activities. We want to replace this habit with a better habit of saving a $100 each month.

So now that we understand habits, what should we do to change this bad habit of spending all of our available money?

The first thing is to identify what habits cause us to spend so much. Is it going out with friends? Is it unnecessary purchases? Exactly what are we spending money on?

The second thing we can do is enlist our rational brain to help overcome our emotional brain. Begin by listing the benefits of saving a $100 each month. This might require a little light research. But just that small effort could help us start saving and result in the following benefits:

- Creating a savings account for emergencies and providing a cushion so a future emergency will not impact our normal lifestyle and routine
- Building overall wealth and reducing life stress
- Investing $100 a month (after having the appropriate savings secured in a bank savings account) could result in about $400,000 at the end of a working career.
- Those who defer spending today can spend even more money and have greater enjoyment in the future.
- People who successfully save and invest typically increase their motivation over time to continue and improve this behavior. I teach in my classes that at first it might seem to be a bit of drudgery to save and invest your $100 each month, but it gets more and more exciting as time passes. You watch your balances grow, and it increases your motivation to save and invest even more money. In other words, you will really like the results it produces and will want more.

The third thing you want to do is to increase your motivation. Do some light research and read about a few people who worked at normal jobs and became financially successful—or in some cases "super" financially successful.

The fourth thing is to develop a strategy to accomplish your habit change. Know that no one jumps from saving nothing each month to saving thousands of dollars the next, so don't try this because it likely won't work. You have to work up to it and build up your savings muscles. The correct strategy is to ease into it over a few weeks or even two or three months.

In this case, our strategy to accomplish our $100-savings-a-month goal is learning what money is dedicated to paying our current bills and what money we have available for discretionary spending. Discretionary money is used for whatever you want each month after all your bills are paid. You have to determine how much discretionary money you have. Once that is done, determine the exact amount you are spending and on what.

To spend less, we must first understand that not all spending brings you the same amount of enjoyment. All spending is not created equal. Look for ways to cut spending that really won't bother you that much—less coffee from Starbucks or reducing the amount of times you eat lunch out—while preserving your spending for what is truly important to you—like maybe saving your money for what you really enjoy, like travel.

Or maybe you can reevaluate your regular monthly bills. For example, if you are renting you might find a cheaper place. How much does where you live really matter to you if it is safe (security) and in a relatively clean area? Do you need a high-end vehicle? A car is just a car to me. I already know that I don't want to spend the time it takes to take care of a really nice car, so I enjoy looking at nice cars but I really don't want one.

Whatever you value or don't value is fine and should guide your spending reduction efforts. Start with the lower-cost items then work your way toward larger expenses to achieve your habit-change goal.

The vehicle example is a good segue. Do you have the habit of always buying a new car after four or five years? Maybe the routine is that every four years you go see your salesperson who makes a big deal out of you coming into the dealership. You get to choose a new car, which is a fun shopping experience, and then you get to drive and be seen in a brand-new car. Here is the habit loop broken down:

1. Cue: You pay off a car.
2. Routine: You go to the dealership and purchase a new vehicle.
3. Reward: You enjoy being made a fuss over by the dealership. You also enjoy shopping for and then driving your new car.

First understand why buying a new car every four or five years is a bad idea. A car loses 33% of its value as soon as it is driven off the lot. There are benefits to saving your car payment rather than buying a new car right away. It would be good to choose a new reward as the change strategy, such as going on a nice vacation (cheaper) rather than buying a new car every four years. You could pocket the extra savings over time. People usually get more satisfaction from experiences over possessions, so this strategy makes perfect sense.

Now, let's switch gears. If you want to create a great new habit to improve your financial life, the very best daily habit to have is to record your spending. This is a key habit or behavior to help you spend less than you make (your larger goal). This way you can easily analyze or evaluate your spending, make decisions about what is important and what can be cut. Once you begin spending less than you make, it changes the entire trajectory of your life for the better.

Take inspiration from people who are rich and still work on their financial lives by controlling their spending. A good example is formula race driver Danica Patrick. She is worth around 60 million, yet she still believes strongly in frugality. In fact, she cooks meals herself rather than eating out whenever she can to both save money and eat healthier.

To create a routine habit of tracking your spending to improve your finances, you need to set up a cue, routine, and reward:

Example: Create the Habit of Recording Your Daily Spending

1. Cue: Before you walk out of the house in the morning, review yesterday's spending.
2. Routine: Record every expense you have in an app or on the notes section of your phone.
3. Reward: Build a reward you enjoy into your budget for success. If you go over your budget, the money for your reward is the first fund to be spent to cover the budget overage.

Then implement your plan, understanding it will likely take in excess of 66 or so days to create an actual habit.

We have covered a lot ground here, so I want to summarize this chapter's change strategies to make it easier for you to utilize them and be successful.

Change Strategies:

1. Identify your current habit loops 1) cue 2) routine and 3) reward.
2. Feed your brain the benefits of creating a new, improved habit.
3. Motivate your brain to move forward by looking at success stories of others who succeeded in changing a similar habit.
4. Develop a reasonable strategy to accomplish your habit change by using one or more of the following strategies:
   A. Replace the habit with a better one.
   B. Change your habit reward.

C. Change your habit routine.

D. The gradual reduction strategy

E. Eliminate habit cues.

  › Lifestyle change strategy to eliminate your habit

F. It will take 66 days or longer to change a habit. Don't give up!

Chapter 4 Summary Formulas

Automatic Pilot Routine + Safety + Conserving Brain Power = Habits

Cue (Start Habit) + Routine (Habit Engaged In) + Reward (Reward Brain Gets) = Habit Loop

Resist Change + Persistent Over Time = Habits

Replace Habit + Substitute Reward + Gradual Reduction + Vacation Strategy + Change Lifestyle = Habit Change Methods

Approx. 66 Days = Successful Habit Change

Define Habit Loop + Change Benefits + Increase Motivation + Clarify Change Strategy = Habit Change

Chapter 5
From Overspending to Financial Freedom

How would you complete the below sentence?

I can simplify my life by _____.

Joann (pseudonym) buys stuff. That is her thing! She buys *a lot* of stuff. She loves buying clothing and various other items for herself. She also buys gifts for her adult kids and even better gifts for her grandchildren. Joann even buys stuff for her friends. The thing is, Joann is deeply in debt. She can barely pay her bills because she buys so much.

Joann also has an extremely stressful job and helps take care of her elderly mother. Joann has been divorced for several years and lives alone. All these stressors frequently overwhelm Joann, and many times, she has absolutely no idea what to do about her problems.

Joann realized this was a bad position to be in, so she set out with the express intention to solve her debt problem. After doing some research to find out how to get out of debt, Joann promptly used her credit card to purchase a cruise to the Bahamas. Joann then went on vacation where she bought even more stuff on credit. No actual financial changes were ever initiated.

Whenever Joann makes purchases it gives her the "relief of spending." This relief takes over for a little while, and she is able to forget about her constant anxiety and stress. Unfortunately, the "relief of spending" is always short lived. The shame and anxiety of creating another bill she can't pay (or can barely pay) restarts her cycle of worry and anxiety all over again. She also has deep shame and remorse whenever she thinks about her finances.

As of this writing, Joann has not overcome her spending or debting behaviors. She still has no specific, workable plan to stop her dysfunctional coping strategy of buying things. Maybe the right incident has not occurred to cause enough discomfort for her to change. The debt Joann incurs now, however, starts to become more and more critical as Joann ages, and her ability to pay off her debt begins to quickly shrink. Joann seems to be headed for disaster as a senior citizen with debt she can't pay and the reduced earning power that comes with aging. Joann's future looks pretty bleak without an emergency intervention.

Her dysfunctional coping strategies make more sense to an outside observer when they learn about her childhood.

Joann grew up poor with a mother and father who were addicted to substances. Before her father passed away, he was an alcoholic and her mother was, and very likely still is, addicted to prescription drugs. Her father worked in construction his entire life, but money was always ebbing and flowing as her father changed jobs frequently. Because both parents struggled with substances and financial issues, Joann was frequently neglected growing up—physically, mentally, and monetarily. These adverse experiences led to not always having enough food or other basic household supplies. When the family had money and her parents were at least semi-sober, Joann was given special treats by her parents—perhaps to assuage their guilt stemming from their substance-induced neglect. Her parents never maintained any savings. Now Joann takes care of her mother (including financially) who is a widow and has no savings to fall back on.

Joann is likely deploying a survival behavior taken from the defective money script that she learned as a child, stemming from her adverse childhood experiences and the emotions that are being trapped inside of her with no place to go. If her parents had money when she was growing up, they may have been happier, and everyone would not have suffered through the constant financial ebb and flow that led to her neglect.

Joann also likely believes she must have things in order to survive. Growing up, she didn't have things. Sometimes that even included food to eat. I can remember a story she told me about putting sugar she found in the cupboard on some very stale bread to have something to eat, or bumming a meal from her next-door neighbors—a very risky strategy because if her parents found out she would be harshly punished. Although she has never specifically told me, Joann is coming from a place of deprivation and fear. The feelings generated from her adverse childhood experiences are also likely the root of Joann feeling powerless, poor and angry about the life she was deprived of and yet desired. These feelings cause her a great deal of pain, and Joann does her best to avoid these feelings by using her money to save both herself and her extended family.

Joann seems to be avoiding her lingering feelings of anger, which is an emotion we were all taught to avoid. When you were young, you were likely taught not to hit others or throw things when you were angry and not to yell at others when your anger became intense. So today, most of us suppress our anger. We certainly do have to control our anger, but anger can be a helpful emotion as well. Anger typically stems from not getting what we need or want. This can lead to greater motivation to obtain the things you are missing or require.

A great story to explain how anger should work in your life is illustrated by a cancer patient I know who is also a nurse. When she received the initial diagnosis and treatment plan, the treatment seemed incongruent with the information and physical evidence she had. She tried to be collegiate with her medical providers and suggested the initial diagnosis might not fit the evidence at hand. She was summarily ignored! This went on until she got angry and began to take charge of her treatment, demanding specific answers about specific physical symptoms and evidence from her providers. She also went around her provider and utilized a different medical team. As it turns out, her initial diagnosis was in fact wrong (later confirmed by her initial medical staff). Although she still has cancer, it is an entirely different cancer with an entirely different treatment regime and a better long-term prognosis. She is now on track with a medical treatment plan that seems to be helping her. If she had not become angry, what would have happened to her? Now when she talks to her providers, they listen very closely to what she has to say. As you can see, anger is a very helpful motivator when it is properly directed and controlled by mature, adult actions.

As I got to know more about Joann, her self-defeating behaviors make more sense. Avoiding her feelings creates a behavior that negatively impacts her finances. As you can see from this common example, the primary problem here is not financial education but the unresolved and emotionally raw life problems that have never been addressed.

Some psychologists have an alternative view of why this particular dysfunctional money script occurs in many people. They believe people like Joann have a behavioral addiction—like gambling for example. The specific name they give to this type of behavioral disorder is Compulsive Buying Disorder (CBD), characterized as an activity a sufferer repeatedly engages in despite negative consequences (extreme debt) and the extensive damage it does to interpersonal relationships (divorce).[1]

Some psychologists believe this is a disorder that is typically found in someone who is simultaneously dealing with several other emotional challenges (called comorbidity in the medical world) such as anxiety, depression, loneliness, low self-esteem, addiction or impulse control. Some believe that CBD is part of a money disorder category called "money worshipping." This category of money disorder includes pathological gambling and workaholism.[2] This alternative view of this behavior contends these conditions are typically found in people with poor personal self-management behaviors who often also suffer from anxiety and depression.

It should be noted that to qualify for this specific diagnosis, you must have had severe consequences or significant damage from your debting behaviors. Of course, this leaves out the millions of people who have a similar problem but have not suffered severe consequences. Yet, they still experience a great deal of shame regarding their spending or debting behaviors. The rigid reference to severe consequences is one reason this theory is not entirely accepted by many psychologists.

The Breakthrough Formula for Prosperity tells us that our life problems are always, unequivocally linked to our finances. If we can find a way to deal with our life problems, our finances improve as well. In this case, there is subconscious anger and resentment holding Joann back from obtaining the life she wants. One of the primary ways we can accomplish prosperity is by reframing our past.

Any debting behaviors we exhibit are just behaviors. They are not us. These behaviors can be addressed and maybe the story and lessons of our past could be reimagined. Don't beat yourself up for your past spending behaviors. After all, nearly two to 16% of our U.S. population is believed to have this particular money issue.[3] That's a lot of people, but the actual number is likely much higher. I base this conclusion on the following: In 2019 the Federal Reserve stated that four out of 10 people could not come up with $400 for emergencies. Also, people in this same group say if they miss a single paycheck, they will be in significant financial trouble and they admitted they would likely skip some payments on their bills at some point in the year.[4]

Now that we understand money scripts better, we can begin to modify our money story to help us control our spending rather than unconsciously harm us. For example, if our problem is spending, we can wake up every morning and repeat one of these mantras:

1. I am safe.
2. I have enough food to eat and clean water to drink.
3. I have clean, reasonably nice clothing to wear.
4. I have a reasonably nice place to live.
5. I don't need anything to be safe or happy.
6. I am enough.
7. I can spoil myself in ways that don't involve money.
8. I can handle feelings of being deprived.
9. I can make good choices.

Incorporate these thoughts into how you view your childhood. "I was financially neglected as a child, but now I am safe!" or "I had a terrible upbringing, but now I don't need anything to be safe and happy." This can help you move forward and stop your unconscious feelings and subsequent behaviors that sabotage your finances and life. *For inspirational stories of people who successfully overcame these debt behaviors, see workbook.*

Speaking of feelings, do you feel anxious with money, avoid necessary spending or constantly worry about the risk of going broke? Do you sometimes neglect your own needs just to save money? Then you'll want to learn about the dangers of underspending and neglecting yourself!

Chapter 5 Summary Formulas

Temporary Excitement +
Stress Relief From Making New Purchases +
Later Regret = CBD

Purchases to Relieve Anxiety +
More Anxiety Due to Later Regret =
Anxiety Disorder

Chapter 6
From Underspending to Financial Security

How would you complete the following sentences?

I feel safe when I _____.
I feel anxious or unsafe when I _____.

D o you feel anxious with money and avoid necessary spending, yet you constantly worry about the risk of going broke? Do you sometimes neglect your own needs just to save money?

When I was a police officer, I was dispatched to an apartment on a check welfare call. This is a type of call where a family member or friend is worried about someone they haven't been able to contact for a while, so they call the police. We were generally sent to the missing person's home.

I had been on hundreds of these types of calls, and on that particular day, I was dispatched to a deteriorating, rough neighborhood. All the large homes on this once-grand street had been split into multiple apartments to create income for their owners. I was met by a landlord who expressed concern that one of his residents had not paid his rent nor had he been seen for several days.

The landlord said this was very unusual behavior for this resident who was always very prompt with the rent. Also, the man was not answering his door. The landlord told me the tenant typically went nowhere and did absolutely nothing. His tenant had no family that he knew of and had no friends that he had ever seen. He was virtually a hermit who rarely left, except to get food. The landlord was actually more concerned for his tenant's welfare, not the rent.

The mail was piling up at the tenant's door—a bad sign. The landlord let me into his apartment. Upon going inside, I found this resident (an older man) had indeed passed away. His body had been there for a week or so. The death, although now hard to tell without coroner analysis, appeared to be of natural causes. So far, this was all very normal.

I summoned the coroner and began searching for information about this resident for the required reports and subsequent death investigation. The apartment was broken up in a very odd manner. It had only a small kitchen downstairs, steep steps upward and a small bathroom and bedroom on the second floor. This small space was sparsely furnished with what appeared to be mismatched, second-hand furniture. The only furniture in the kitchen was a very old wooden desk and a chair shoved up against a bare wall opposite the kitchen cabinetry. The bedroom had a single bed, a nightstand, and a dresser with an ancient TV sitting on top of it with rabbit ears protruding from its top.

The furniture was covered in dust. The apartment was not cluttered, however, because this man had no possessions with which to clutter it. He had little clothing in the closet and a few kitchen dishes and utensils. This appeared to be a very financially poor man with no family who was living meagerly in this tiny apartment on Social Security. I began looking for his ID card to verify his identify and search for his next of kin. I first looked in the kitchen's desk. The first thing I came across was an old bank savings book with deposit statements inside of it. It had a written balance of $250,000 in it. That was very unusual! Then I found another bank book listing an entirely different account, with yet another $250,000 in it. Then I found another and then another and another. Soon, all the accounts totaled over three million dollars!

It was difficult to wrap my head around the situation. The man appeared to be living in poverty, but he could afford anything he wanted. With that kind of money he could go anywhere or do almost anything. Yet, instead, he lived alone like a hermit with only his various bank accounts to keep him company.

The man was likely an underspender. Trusting others with money (or perhaps anything else) is very difficult for underspenders. I've known other underspenders who lived entirely without any serious romantic companionship for this exact reason. They could not bring themselves to share or trust others with their hard-earned money. In this case, the rich hermit's closest acquaintance seemed to be his landlord. The landlord would collect the rent in person monthly, and the two of them always chatted for a while.

The follow-up investigation eventually revealed the rich tenant was a retired executive at a medical insurance corporation in Ohio. He had likely made a lot of money over his career and evidently saved every last dime of his wages. He was so miserly with his money he would not even invest it to create more wealth because he might lose some of it. He likely kept his savings accounts to $250K because this is the top limit for which the federal government will ensure a depositor's savings. He had many accounts, so he could keep them at this magic limit. He must have felt his money was safe and insured. Later, I learned that the rich tenant had even more millions than I had found on my cursory search of his desk drawer.

According to the coroner, this man died of a chronic medical condition, and he was not getting the proper treatment for his condition. Properly treating a chronic medical condition would cost him money, after all. Clearly, such action was a nonstarter for this wealthy hermit. So he died alone, without friends, with few acquaintances, and no one to love or be loved by. In my opinion, that's a tragedy. He had left a proper will and gave all of his money to a local university. It was great that he was able to help others with his money after he passed away but such a shame that he couldn't squeeze a little living into his life.

I was not able to learn anything about the wealthy hermit's background or childhood, but likely he came from a home with scarce financial resources. Or perhaps his parents exhibited similar types of behavior. I talked with one underspender—who I will call Mark—who said when he was growing up, his dad was extremely miserly. His dad hoarded money and kept it away from everyone else in the family—even from his wife and kids. Worse, Mark told me his father would take his (Mark's) personal money and keep it whenever he got the slightest opportunity to do so. Mark's dad would tell Mark he would deposit his son's cash in the bank for him, then later his dad would pretend to know nothing about the money Mark had given to him. His dad would also borrow money from Mark. Of course, the father would keep the money and never pay Mark back. Mark soon learned to hide his money from his dad and the rest of his family.

Mark has also grown up to be a committed underspender—no big surprise there. Although Mark says his behavior is not nearly as severe as his father's, the behavior is still noticeable. Mark has anxiety surrounding spending his money. He also still harbors significant resentment toward his father and his father's constant betrayal of his trust. As an adult, Mark now hoards money in both his bank accounts and also has created hidden cash stashes around his home. However, Mark tries very hard to not neglect the needs of his family.

People from backgrounds like Mark's sometimes develop underspending behaviors. They think nothing of neglecting their own basic needs like food, clothing, and shelter. Sometimes, as we have illustrated, they will even neglect the needs of their family to save money.[1] By engaging in miserly behaviors, the underspender creates feelings of safety and security by hoarding cash. They feel they must do this because they are terrified of running out of money or going bankrupt, no matter how illogical that might be. Saving gives them relief from this anxiety. Their internal money stories include:

- I can never have enough money.
- More money will make me safe.
- I will be in physical danger without money.
- More money will make me happier.
- Money is a scarce resource needed for survival.
- If I spend any of my money today, I might need it later.
- I might go bankrupt.

Although underspenders might be happy with their extreme miserly behaviors, their family and friends are typically not happy with them at all. Like my friend Mark mentioned above, his dad's behavior created long-term resentment and roadblocks to close family relationships. Mark said his dad continued his severe underspending behavior until the day he passed away.

I have had several coworkers who are underspenders. I have watched one spend hours and hours trying to repair his ancient vehicle. I am never for wasting money, my car has over 100,000 miles on it, but your time is also valuable. It would have made much more sense financially for him to buy a newer, used vehicle at a frugal price and spend his extra time at work making more money.

Remember, as our Breakthrough Formula for Prosperity clearly demonstrates, money behaviors rarely have anything to do with math. Money behaviors are intricately entangled in your life's past challenges, current life stressors and money habits. Although the underspenders have many good money habits, they fail to deal with their past and the life problems that grew from their past.

The Breakthrough Formula for Prosperity also points out that if you have persistent money problems, you generally have persistent life problems as well. For example, underspenders usually alienate those around them and destroy family relationships. I have also seen the damage severe underspending does to their children first-hand. They usually seem to grow up and have a similar money story (remember the witch's curse). The money story is that they value security, safety and relief from anxiety. That relief has been linked to saving every dime they can save.

To change this money script, we have to reframe what we have learned and how we recall our past history and money lessons. For example, you can reframe the lessons you learned about saving money being good to:

1. Having nice things or taking care of myself does not harm myself or others.
2. Everyone deserves a warm, safe, and clean place to live.

3. Feeling angry is okay because I can channel anger to create positive change in my life.
4. I deserve good things in life.
5. I deserve good medical care.
6. I deserve to be happy and have meaningful relationships with others.
7. I deserve to live a fulfilling life.

The education component of the Breakthrough Formula for Prosperity shows us that hoarding piles of cash (or keeping it in the bank) does not necessarily equate to greater survival, safety or even security. Although money absolutely helps with many issues, it does nothing at all for many other aspects of life. Money cannot protect you from heartache, loneliness, disappointment, cancer, domestic turmoil, poor health, being struck by a drunk driver, the collapse of society or even from being randomly murdered as you walk down the street.

One of the biggest tragedies in the lives of the poor is they live their lives without the full texture of life experiences and joy that financial resources could provide them. Underspenders, who have plenty of financial resources, suffer the exact same fate. But underspenders have little interest in any life experiences should they cost even a few pennies. The underspender's mind is mired within a prison of money scarcity, deprivation and desire for safety rather than the feelings of joy, abundance and the freedom that financial resources should provide those fortunate enough to have it.

Of course, this is not how underspenders see themselves. Their self-view is they live in virtuous frugality while avoiding needless, imprudent expenses. They are perfectly happy with their underspending, while they typically alienate everyone who is close to them with their severe miserly behaviors.

Can an underspender ever change? (*See workbook for more information.*) I'll share a story told to me by a close friend about an underspender changing his behavior:

"My father has three million dollars in assets which he made by optioning 3M stock when he was a young man. He also secured a lot of 3M stock at six dollars a share when he was a 3M employee. When he and my mom needed to go into a nursing home they bargain shopped for the best price. They said they would be more comfortable in a home that wasn't so fancy. I had to move them twice before they understood that using their hard-earned money to care for themselves would mean better-trained staff, better living conditions and, most importantly, better food!

"When it was time to sign the paperwork for this last move, my dad was struggling with the price tag. I had to push him to do it. I told him that they could not take their money with them, and that their children are perfectly okay with even a fraction of what they had worked so hard to make and save.

"His decision to sign the papers meant that my mother was very well cared for during the last 11 months of her life. She died clean, fed and in peace. Dad is thriving in this new environment, even though it comes with a very large price tag.

"Has this experience changed his thought processes or attitude? He still needed to be nudged a few days ago to purchase a new mattress, even though his old mattress was causing him back pain. In the end, not a lot of change has occurred."

As is true with all of us, you can only change how you think and your behaviors if you feel there is a need to change. Change for underspenders seems to be very difficult unless they are ready for a significant change in thinking.

Consider this challenge: Can you go to the doctor for a checkup or to get a persistent medical problem checked? If the idea is abhorrent to you or causes you great anxiety, then you are very likely an underspender. If it causes you anxiety, then you obviously need to set a goal with a deadline to get a proper checkup. Remember, money can't help you if you don't use it to benefit your health.

With all the issues we now understand that we carry around about relating to our money, can you imagine the explosive mix of trying to add two different money stories together? Just think of all the problems this will cause. In most partnerships, this is by far the biggest point of conflict. Keep reading to learn how to overcome your ongoing domestic money battles.

Chapter 6 Summary Formulas

Extreme Financial Saver + Depriving Themselves + Depriving Their Family = Underspender

Extreme Underspending + Lack of Trust In Others = Poor Romantic & Family Relationships

Lack of Positive Life Experiences + Lack of Life Fulfillment + Mindset of Scarcity = The Unlived Life

Chapter 7
From Financial Infidelity to Relationship Harmony

How would you complete the below sentences?

I avoid conflicts at home because _____
_____.

I like to avoid conflicts at work because _____
_____.

Our joint, long-term goals are _____
_____.

I have a friend, who I'll call Jim, who owns his own carpet cleaning company. He retired from his day job and is now running this small business to create an additional income stream. The last time he was cleaning our carpets, Jim told me he is going to break up with his long-term, cohabitating girlfriend. He was emotional to the point of choking up as he spoke. With red, blurry eyes he told me how distraught he was over this situation. He said he was sick with disappointment and grief over his dying relationship. He said he now harbors resentment from her betrayal of his trust via her secret spending.

Jim feels likes he works hard to bring an additional income stream into their household while budgeting his other income streams in an attempt to fund their life. His girlfriend, however, has been (in his view) sabotaging his financial efforts. He has talked with her about her spending and explained why they must do their best to stay within their budget. She readily agrees during their budget discussions, but then she secretly begins spending behind his back. If asked during casual conversation, she will deny she is spending money. Only after being confronted with proof will she even begin to discuss it.

His girlfriend also uses every opportunity to secure cash from their family budget so she can spend without being monitored. Jim said he has done everything from begging her to stop her secret spending to giving her relationship ultimatums. Nothing has worked for more than a few days. He now says he can't see any other option but breaking up with her. In fact, as Jim has shared with me previously, her spending was the very reason he had been cautious about marrying her earlier in their relationship.

In another example, when I was on a vacation in Las Vegas I was drinking a cola and having a snack in a cafe attached to a large casino. I watched and listened as a woman next to me borrowed money from her friend on the phone so she could cover up a large gambling payout she didn't want her husband to find out about. Any sympathy I might have felt for her getting carried away with her gambling immediately evaporated as I watched her return to the gaming tables right after she borrowed money from her friend.

One of my coworkers confided in me that she kept her finances separate from her husband's income. However, her husband had gone into so much debt he could no longer pay his part of their joint monthly bills. She was forced to help bail him out by paying his part their household bills or they'd be behind on their debts and monthly expenses. Her husband's persistent, secretive spending was why she had insisted keeping their finances separate to begin with. In retrospect, keeping their finances separate did not seem to help her very much.

These are all examples of financial infidelity. Financial infidelity is when a spouse or partner makes secret purchases, spends hidden money, keeps assets secret, or generally hides financial actions from their partner, particularly when they know their partner would not approve. More severe cases involve secret credit card accounts, a spouse hiding assets and even secret second mortgages on the couple's home.

You might think that in comparison to these stories, making occasional purchases and hiding them from your partner isn't really so bad. But remember relationships, romantic or otherwise, are built upon a foundation of trust. Trust is hard to rebuild once it is damaged. If you get caught a few times hiding purchases from your partner, he or she might simply be angry with you. Sooner or later, however, making secret purchases or other secret financial moves will erode trust that is vital to your relationship.

If you begin to lose trust in your partner because of various lies about his or her finances, your partner will likely then think, *What else are you lying to me about?*

The number-one, most common reason people engage in secret spending is to avoid conflict.[1] One person is being conflict avoidant and doesn't want to have an honest discussion and suffer the fallout surrounding a purchase their partner does not approve of. However, there are other reasons people lie to their partners about money. Here are some other reasons I have heard from friends, family and coworkers:

- Giving one of their children money when the spouse would not approve of this gift
- Romantic affair(s)
- One plans to divorce the other and is hiding assets
- A second family (yes, this actually happens)
- Giving money to someone (not their partner) because they are emotionally connected to them, romantically or otherwise
- Drug addiction
- Gambling addiction
- Paying a prostitute for sex
- The stress relief found in the "relief of spending"

Could your partner be hiding money issues or spending? According to a report from National Public Radio (NPR), 41% of spouses are hiding spending, lying about spending or even have secret loans or bank accounts. In fact, NPR notes financial infidelity is slightly more common than sexual infidelity, and men are statistically the greatest offenders.[2]

Lying about money is a common way people sabotage their financial futures. It keeps us not only poor in the present but likely will keep us poor in the immediate future as well. Financial infidelity not only sabotages the offender but also their partner's financial future without the partner's knowledge, which is a significant breach of trust. This harms relationships financially and emotionally and is dysfunctional behavior that needs to be addressed as soon as possible.

One of the basic premises of the Breakthrough Formulas for Prosperity indicates that if your partner is habitually lying to you about spending, he or she likely has other life problems that need to be addressed as well. According to the ACEs study discussed in previous chapters, as in most persistent, dysfunctional money behaviors, our childhood money story impacts our current view of the world. Past adverse childhood events create subconscious beliefs that lead to our behaviors and our daily habits.

Psychology Today says avoiding conflict stems from having internal anxiety or fear of upsetting others. During childhood, the conflict-avoiders likely had parents who physically bullied, scorned them or were harshly critical of their actions and words.[3] Because of the secret spender's challenging past, he or she likely became fearful of conflict due to accompanying emotional rejection or even physical abuse that followed any parental conflict.[4] As a child in a hostile or caustic environment, this was likely a good strategy—or at least as good as any other strategy in such a toxic environment. As an adult, however, this strategy is significantly dysfunctional and leads to heartache.

The Breakthrough Formula for Financial Prosperity has shown repeatedly that most consistent money problems are really the result of life problems that also happen to impact our finances. The formula predicts that being conflict-avoidant in domestic financial matters as an adult will be a pervasive behavior found across multiple areas of life. Likely, the secret spender is conflict-avoidant at work and with their friends as well.

Being conflict-avoidant damages the spender's job performance, finances, future, their spouse and even their current self-esteem. It creates shame and self-loathing, which reaffirms the messages the conflict-avoider likely heard from his or her parents as a child. For example, the secret spender has less worth than others and "doesn't deserve good things."

If you are married to someone who has committed financial infidelity, you cannot insult, yell or harass your partner into better money behaviors. He or she is a separate person who you cannot control, at least not for very long, as their behavior has already proven. Giving someone serious heat, especially a conflict-avoidant personality, for not living up to the budget might work in the short term, but it will never create the lasting changes you need. Instead, you will have to draw out your partner to get their true opinion(s), wants and desires. Inevitable conflict must not be seen as win-or-lose proposition by you, but a way to find the path forward.

If you are the secret spender, you are going to have to stop agreeing with your spouse to avoid conflicts. Conflict in all relationships is inevitable. You are going to have to step up and be heard—in a mature, adult fashion. Your conflict avoidance strategy is clearly not working and is sabotaging both your life and your relationship.

The Breakthrough Formula demonstrates the best way for both partners to find harmony in a relationship is to get on the same page. Getting on the same page begins with a discussion of long-term, mid-term and short-term goals *(see workbook)*. If the goals are both valued and shared, both people will be willing to work and sacrifice to obtain them. If they are not, it will be a difficult journey forward. It is essential that both spouses participate and share their goals during this discussion.

Next, the goal must be to demonstrate the behavior you want to see from your partner with your own actions. You also need to be positive and able to freely discuss money issues without getting upset, accusatory or trying to skirt the truth. If you fail to demonstrate the behavior you want to see, your efforts will have little influence over your partner and will be seen as "do as I say and not as I do." All of us are typically great at finding behaviors that need improvement with our partners, but not always so great at recognizing our own errant behavior. You should try to be bulletproof in areas of budgeting, spending and saving if you want your partner to be the same.

When we are more attuned to our own behaviors, we can then begin to try to influence the behavior of our significant other. Gráinne M. Fitzsimons and Eli J. Finkel have researched the area of partner motivation thoroughly and can provide us the education we need to succeed. They conclude that it is possible to increase your significant other's commitment to your shared goals—assuming you both did the work together to create shared goals.[5] The strategies you use, however, are very important. You are trying to motivate your significant other. Motivation, just like at work, is best accomplished by thoroughly explaining the benefits of achieving the goal and then both encouraging and recognizing your partner's progress toward achieving your shared vision. After all, you share this vision, and you should both feel excitement for it. Give praise and recognition for his or her efforts regularly.

Also, be forgiving! We all make mistakes and have epic failures. Treat your significant other like you would want to be treated if you'd made a mistake. Speaking harshly or belittling your partner will create resentments, increase conflict and create bitterness that will live long after this particular issue is forgotten.

Another leadership principle is helping your partner to develop strategies to improve his or her performance. If your partner will accept it, provide this assistance on strategies in a positive, subtle manner. If he or she starts to get resentful, lay off the issue for a bit. Let it be known that you are there to help and wait for your partner to approach you. Don't overly intrude into your significant other's behaviors. If your help is not requested or wanted when it is offered, this will only lead to increased resentment and further relationship obstacles. You have already discussed the monthly budget spending parameters when they were initially set. Wait until the end of the month to make any comments, and phrase your inquiry in the following manner, "How can I help you achieve _____?"

If one spouse does not value the process and the outcome of controlling your joint spending, saving and working toward goals, then the two of you have much less of a chance of successfully altering your current behaviors to achieve the goals you set. The further spouses' motivation moves away from them personally desiring both the process and the outcomes, the less likely it is that the two of them can succeed.[6] You overcome this reluctance with getting your partner to set a goal and commit to the outcomes he or she deeply desires that would be made possible by improving your joint finances. That will increase the intrinsic motivation to accomplish the goal.

What if your spouse isn't earning enough money or not contributing an equal share to your household income? What can you do you if the non-contributing spouse is you? Keep reading to learn how to tackle the problem of under earning.

Chapter 7 Summary Formulas

Secret Spending + Secret Credit Card Bills + Hiding Purchases + Secret Loans = Financial Infidelity

Agreed-upon Goals + Support for Spouse + Forgiveness + Cooperation + Strategies to Improve Performance = Increased Commitment to Family Budget

Chapter 8
From Under-Earning to Joyous Work

How would you answer the following questions?

Do you enjoy your job?
Are you earning a competitive wage for the work you do?
Can you come up with three additional ways to make more money?

A story that explains underearning perfectly is that of my friend, who we will call Dave. Dave is an attorney. Notice I didn't say a successful attorney. Dave has his own independent practice and specializes in estate planning and writing wills. He doesn't have an office or an office staff, which is not necessarily a bad thing. The problem, though, is that Dave doesn't have a lot of clients. What Dave does have, however, is school debt!

Dave always wanted to be an attorney from the time he was able to think about a career path. He attended a private, expensive university for both his undergraduate and subsequent law degree. Although his parents paid a great deal of it, his student loan bill is still huge. Luckily, he lives alone, lives extremely modestly, and makes ends meet—most of the time. Many times, Dave is not able to pay all his monthly bills on time or in full. When talking with Dave, I don't really get the sense that he understands his finances very well. He does not have a lot of confidence in his financial abilities and frequently says, "I don't know anything about money!" His life always seems to be in some type of financial or personal chaos.

Dave is a very frustrating friend, and I must admit that I did lose track of him over the years. Dave only made enough money to get by—some months not even that much. He usually ended up working only 12 to 15 hours a week. He primarily writes wills. Since wills can also be downloaded from the internet and can even be self-filed in probate court, his list of potential clients is limited to those who are uncomfortable with that process or have a situation they feel is too complicated for the internet route. This is obviously not a large nor a particularly affluent client pool.

I fully admit, due to my childhood upbringing, I have a rescue personality. So naturally, I came up with numerous suggestions to help Dave expand his client base and thereby increase his income, like advertising his estate planning service to police officers. Dave dismissed all of my ideas as soon as they came out of my mouth. I also come across many people who ask me if I knew a good attorney, but it soon became apparent Dave didn't really want referrals from me. Referrals meant Dave might have to go to court. Dave hated going to court!

In short, Dave only seemed to want to work within his own set, narrow range. He wanted to handpick his clients and cases—mainly wills and estate planning. He wasn't interested in trying anything new. All that would have been perfectly fine if he was happy with his situation. However, Dave regularly complained about his lack of income and struggled mightily to pay his sizable student loan bill. He also struggled with keeping his older Mercedes running. Dave tried to project success, but when you scratched the surface, you soon learned how much he was struggling financially. Dave was a classic underearner.

Underearning is a tricky issue, according to Michelle Bohls. "Those who under earn usually deny they are doing so," she says. Often times they pretend they are much more successful than they actually are in order to avoid being judged by others. Almost always, they are earning and working under their real potential.[1]

Underearning might seem on the surface to be a symptom of depression and not necessarily an underearning mindset. One way to tell the difference is that underearners work for little pay and yet fail to make earning more money a priority. At the same time, they are embarrassed to ask for what they are rightfully owed or for the pay they deserve.[2] Underearners typically work hard, but their pay doesn't meet their needs or usually even the normally accepted pay rate for their work. Frequently, they find themselves doing work for free.[3]

Underearners are also similar to underachievers. The difference is, underachievers may never reach their full potential but their income could be fine for their needs and they are not embarrassed to ask for more pay or what they are owed.[4]

Frequently, the background of underearners is they have not mentally separated themselves from their families' wealth.[5] For example, I know a young man who works and earns very little. His entire plan in life is to wait until his very rich mother dies and leaves him a very large trust fund that was set up by his late father. In the interim, he works at several jobs and receives minimum pay. He is not really concerned about making money. No worries there, as his mom helps him out with his monthly bills.

Some underearners come from a background where they were harshly criticized at home. They now lack self-confidence or subconsciously feel inferior. This attitude, when combined with a money-is-a-scarce-commodity mindset, limits the underearners' ability to see options and choices that could help them change their lives for the better. They seem blocked from envisioning different possibilities or alternative courses of action to become more prosperous.[6] *Take the test in workbook to see if you are an underearner.*

The Breakthrough Formula for Prosperity shows us that we have the best chance of success when we educate ourselves. In this case, learn about money mindsets. A money-is-a-scarce-commodity mindset is a belief that money is a rare resource that people must struggle and compete for. Those with a scarcity mindset believe there is never enough money to go around to meet their needs—they must work and scrounge and develop a wait-and-see-how-things-develop attitude. A scarcity mindset also supports a belief that rich people are greedy and take more than their fair share. This mindset is usually associated with a fear of financial failure.[7]

In an abundant mindset, the mindset of the rich, you embrace money and your need for it in your life. You see money as a resource that is available to anyone who wants to put forth the effort to get it. You are excited about the limitless possibilities open to you for success and you understand you are only limited by your thinking and creativity. You want to take charge of your life and move forward. You firmly believe that those who seek prosperity can have it.[8]

The scarcity or abundant mindsets are particularly pertinent for those who work for themselves in their own businesses. Time and time again, I have seen talented experts who habitually charge less than the prevailing price for their services. Even though their work or services are superior, they are uncomfortable charging more. If someone balks, the underearner immediately drops their price with little negotiation.

Our Breakthrough Formula for Prosperity tells us that if a person has persistent money issues, it is typically a symptom of additional, serious life problems as well. Underearning is no exception. Underearning impacts every aspect of your life, from the daily financial chaos it creates to self-sabotage behaviors at work—such as making less than competitive wages. Typically, underearners are undervalued by their employers, likely because they have already undervalued themselves at work.[9] Usually, underearners have a, "poverty is noble" or an "I hate those greedy rich" frame of mind.[10]

Maintaining domestic relationships is very difficult for underearners, as fighting about money is one of the top predictors of future divorce.[11] Under-contributing to the household income is a huge stressor in marriages. Marriages can begin to fray when one partner is perceived as not contributing to the financial wellbeing of the partnership. As with most past money stories that are not serving our needs, we need to alter our past money story to create better beliefs, behaviors and outcomes in the present. Underearners are stuck in a money-is-scarce mindset. We must reframe our money story in a way that fuels better beliefs and then creates better behaviors and habits. We need to alter our thoughts to a money-is-abundant mindset. It all starts with altering the lessons you have learned about money growing up, in addition to taking on whichever of the following mantra(s) apply to you.

1. I deserve to be financially successful.
2. I deserve to be happy and rich.
3. Me being happy and having good things in life hurts no one else.

4. Those who love me want me to be prosperous and happy.
5. I am worthy.
6. I am good enough.
7. I am competent and talented and deserve good pay.
8. I deserve, just like everyone else, to be paid fairly for my talents and work.
9. I can financially help others if I am financially successful.
10. Working for free devalues my great talents and abilities.
11. I have dreams and a vision I can accomplish.
12. I trust myself to take only what is fair.
13. I have every reason to have confidence in myself and my abilities.
14. Money is plentiful for those who want it.
15. Why not me?
16. I can succeed financially.

The Breakthrough Formula also explains that we can envision a new, better life by, in part, setting goals to create the life that we both want and deserve to have. We can start with increasing our annual earnings. The idea is to stretch your abilities to make it challenging, but not impossible. There is a sweet spot.

This problem of underearning is so common, there is even an organization dedicated to helping underearners overcome their current limitations in thinking and behavior. Underearners Anonymous underearnersanonymous.org is a program that evolved from Spenders Anonymous (spendersanonymou.com) and Debtors Anonymous (debtorsanonymous.com). It is based on the 12-step model which strives to change member behavior through the process of group support and modeling more adaptive financial behaviors. Underearners Anonymous has a history of success for those who take to the system.

Underearning is a significant life problem that impacts everything from your financial standing to your family relationships. If you want to change this behavior, the first step is altering your money story or script to enable you to change your money mindset. The second step is to educate yourself about an abundant mindset. The third step is to set your goals and increase your financial earnings every year.

If you really want to earn more money, be more successful and maybe even become wealthy, then you also need to know about financial planning and its impact upon your life. Keep reading to learn more about the vital skill of financial planning.

Chapter 8 Summary Formulas

Working Below Ability +
Working For Less Pay + Scarcity Mindset +
Lack of Financial Confidence = Underearning

Reframing Money Story +
Increasing Self-Confidence +
Abundant Mindset + Financial Education +
Goal Setting = Improved Earning Ability

Chapter 9
From Money Avoidance to Embracing Financial Planning

How would you complete the below sentence?

I avoid working on my budget because _____.

This is the painfully true story about one of my readers who later became a friend who I'll call June. She was happily married for about 20 years. She and her husband had two wonderful boys. June's husband was a great guy who had a good job in a higher management position at a large company that paid him well. Her husband was very good with money; June was not. Her husband gladly took care of all the bills, the investing and even the family's household budget. June was comfortable with that because she felt she was never good with money and her husband was extremely talented in this area. She had no problem following the budgetary directions of her husband if it meant she did not have to be involved with the household budget. The couple soon became wealthy due to her husband's significant salary, talent with money and his investing savvy.

June and her husband developed a circle of friends, all upper-middle class, who lived in and around a their very nice neighborhood. June would meet with a group of wives on certain mornings and they would all go walking together. They formed an informal, morning fitness club and a close bond as time passed.

All things considered, June's family was doing well in almost all aspects of life and the family was thriving.

As often happens, things change. June's husband suddenly came down with brain cancer and passed away in only a few short months from his disease. June was devastated by this loss. Her friends at the informal fitness club circled around her and gave her emotional and moral support during her husband's illness and after his death. The ladies demonstrated outright love and compassion for her loss and her new situation. She felt truly lucky to have such friends to help her through a difficult time in her life. This made the group even closer.

Once on her own, June discovered (or more accurately rediscovered) that she was anxious about her money and personal finances. The family was in great financial shape, but she felt anxious every time she even thought about the family's large financial resources. She had no idea how to create or maintain a family budget, let alone deal with a complicated investment portfolio her husband had accumulated and left to her. Therefore, June delayed doing anything.

June shared her financial concerns with her morning fitness group. Once again, this group immediately jumped to June's rescue involving their husbands, many of whom were financial investment brokers and investment bankers. She trusted her friends explicitly, and by default, her friends' husbands. June eagerly turned over her finances to these men and returned to her safe world of financial avoidance.

Things didn't go well after that. Soon, money began disappearing in June's accounts at an alarming rate. Some of it was lost in various inappropriate investments, some of it was spent in financial fees and some just disappeared, and June had no idea what happened to it. It took her a while to notice the problem, and soon the family was struggling financially. It was so bad she contacted an attorney who immediately filed several civil lawsuits against her friends' spouses. Some of the family's money was eventually restored—but not all of it. June was also assigned a financial guardian by the court due to her dismal financial performance. The guardian now tightly controls this family's finances.

June was devastated by what she felt was a total betrayal of her trust, affection and what she thought was the loyalty of her friends. June has gone on to make new friends and the family is moving past this difficult financial and emotional trauma. Everyone seems to be doing reasonably well after these life altering incidents, but resentments and mistrust of others remain ingrained into this family's altered personality.

Besides being a reminder that friends and money don't always mix well, this story brings home the potential dangers surrounding the self-defeating behaviors of financial avoidance. Financial avoidance, as this story demonstrates, creates landmines in the future that explode and create significant financial and life destructing events. Most people believe only those who have meager financial means avoid dealing with their money issues. As June's story shows, financial avoidance is not limited to low-income individuals. It can be found across all social classes.

In fact, a 2020 study found that 77% of Americans believe they can't effectively control their finances. Worse yet, this same group believes that their money problems actually control them![1] Another 2020 survey, published in mint.com reports that 59% of the U.S. population is living paycheck to paycheck and carrying an average credit card balance of $8,398 month to month.[2]

Money avoidance is a dysfunctional, emotional coping mechanism that encapsulates your inner, subconscious beliefs about money—primarily that money is a bad thing, money is evil or it corrupts those who have it.[3] All of these feelings stem, once again, from the experiences you have incorporated into your money story in childhood that were later modified by more recent money experiences.

There are many different types of self-sabotaging financial behaviors that involve money avoidance. The particular relevant subcategories of money avoidance discussed in this chapter include the specific behaviors related to financial denial and financial rejection.[4]

Financial denial is brought on by what the sufferer believes will be an uncomfortable or emotionally painful financial situation when they finally examine their finances.[5] For many people, it is much easier for them to avoid or even deny a problem exists rather than face the emotional turmoil of examining their financial status and feeling the emotions this process will bring to the surface. They desperately want to avoid feeling like a failure and feeling shame, fear and a subconscious confirmation that they are inadequate or will never be "enough."

When the sufferer tries to avoid or ignore their financial problems to circumvent their inner negative feelings and associations, it creates even more stress surrounding their money issues. This is because the full scope of the problem is unknown to the sufferer. This leaves the subsequent fallout to their imagination or worst nightmares. Later, when the problem must finally be understood and handled, the sufferer typically reacts with extreme panic and maximum stress.[6]

Money rejection is slightly different, but still a very common subcategory of money avoidance. It involves the outright rejection of money. Some people have been taught since childhood that those who have money are greedy or just plain bad people. Also, money rejection is prevalent in those with low self-esteem and minimal confidence in their own financial abilities. Such feelings have sometimes been linked with receiving an inheritance and the loss of a loved one—when the heir of the inheritance has been taught that money is bad. Consider the story of Kathy Trant. Trant lost her husband in the 9-11 Twin Towers terrorist attack. As a result, she received millions in compensation.[7] The money didn't help her much emotionally, however, and Trant spiraled into depression caused by her overwhelming grief. Trant also immediately blew through five-million dollars by buying luxury ocean cruises for her friends, giving her money away and buying lavish gifts for herself. Further, researchers now say this was actually a very common behavior of those who lost loved ones in the 9-11 disaster and later received millions in compensation. Obviously, these grieving people have a lot going on emotionally with grief, loss and what this event represented to their subconscious.

Common subconscious money scripts for money avoidance include:

- The rich are greedy and take advantage of others.
- It is virtuous to be poor.
- Why do I deserve money when others do not have it?
- I am a money failure.
- I am no good with money.[8]

Here are some examples of the outward behaviors associated with financial rejection and financial avoidance:

- Extreme effort to avoid thinking about their finances
- Giving away money when they can't afford to
- Paying the bills of other people
- Piling up unopened bank statements and bills
- Ignoring all matters financial
- Relief of spending behaviors
- Not budgeting
- Not saving
- Charging large amounts on credit then making only the minimum payments
- Avoid talking about money
- Compulsively getting rid of their money through frivolous spending[9]

Money avoiders (those who have money rejection behaviors) and those with general money anxiety can begin creating the outcomes they want by reframing their unconscious money beliefs. All the negative money scripts and stories we tell ourselves about money was simply something we were taught as children.[10] They are not true. Altering these scripts to create better outcomes has repeatedly proven to be a successful way of beginning to reprogram our subconscious money behaviors.

As an example, we can reframe our money story by saying the following: "I had a rough start, but…

- it hurts no one else for me to have the financial resources I need to enjoy my life."
- I am now improving my ability to manage money."
- I am now pretty good at money management."
- I am now learning to financially plan."
- I am using a financial plan to build prosperity."

The primary means of gaining control of your financial life is the process of financial planning. When I say "financial planning," 77% of my readers will panic. Even the thought of working through a financial plan and the related steps is enough to send us running over the nearest cliff. Breathe deeply and stay with me. I can get you there without a full-blown panic attack. *(For further information on creating a low-stress plan, see workbook section on financial planning.)*

A financial plan is just a document—a piece of paper. You can and will create this document yourself. A financial plan includes a summary of your current financial situation, a budget and your life plans. It lists your short- and long-term goals and outlines your plan to reach those goals. If you are worried, take heart, none of this is nearly as complicated as it seems.

Most people think of a financial plan as a budget, but a budget is just one tool inside your larger financial plan. A financial plan is the underpinning document that we produce so we understand how to achieve our life's financial goals. This is how we fit everything together. Anyone serious about financial freedom needs to create a financial plan.

A financial plan typically has these five components:

1. A person's current financial situation (net worth)
2. Long-term financial goals
3. A plan to achieve your goals
4. Budget
5. A method to monitor your progress

The process of financial planning can change almost everything in your life for the better, both psychologically and monetarily.

The psychological benefits to a financial plan include getting you to think about your long-term goals. Thinking about long-term goals, even for short period of time, has been shown in various studies to reduce your financial stress and create abstract thinking behaviors.[11] Abstract thinking behaviors are highly desirable because it makes it easier to create prosperity. Abstract thinkers are more willing to delay financial spending/gratification to a later date to meet their current goals, while a concrete thinker has more difficulty with this behavior.[12] The point is, those with financial anxiety can overcome these behaviors, save more money and make their lives prosperous by making it a point to concentrate on their long-term financial goals.[13]

As an important side note, saving money has also been shown to have a therapeutic and calming impact that reduces both financial and general life anxiety. It has also been shown to reduce the level of anxiety about the future by reducing a person's "what if" thinking.[14]

A financial plan simply explains how we are going to direct the money flowing into our lives to best support the direction we want to go and to achieve the goals we have chosen to pursue—like those named in the previous chapter, for example. Nearly all of life's goals require a financial component to support them.

In the financial plan we are going to create, we shoot for big outcomes that support our goals. To accomplish our goals, however, we start by first setting and achieving our smaller sub-goals—such as saving money and reducing our debt this week. Then we move on to setting monthly, quarterly and annual goals, then your larger goals for life.

All financial planning ultimately contains a component for creating savings. The best tool for creating savings at the end of the month is, and always will be, the budget.

Total Monthly Income - Total Monthly Expenses = Monthly Profit or Savings

Let me give you a different perspective on saving money. Did you know when all is said and done, individuals aren't much different from businesses? Companies must produce a profit! If they do not produce a profit, they have to quickly make the needed changes to remain viable. If they are not profitable, they could face a shutdown. Individuals face this exact same issue. Everyone, whether they understand it or not, is essentially a "Me Incorporated." At our house, we call it "Faulkner Incorporated." Just like any other business, you can't go deeper and deeper into debt in your monthly, quarterly, and annual profit statements and remain solvent—at least not for long—before going bankrupt. If you are operating in the red, you must immediately make changes and become solvent quickly.

Like any other business, Me Inc. will have to analyze income numbers and monthly, quarterly and annual expenses. You then analyze your budget and figure how to be more profitable. By doing this, you are in fact, creating your financial plan.

- Do I make a profit each month (savings)?
- What changes can I make to become more profitable?
- What is my largest expense category and how can I reduce it?
- What can I cut without noticing it much?
- What can I live without temporarily to increase my profitability?
- Long-term, how can I reduce my expenses to increase profits?

- Can I increase income or save money to cover expected shortfalls in profit?
- How can I use my monthly profits to create even more profits (investing)?

Companies that break even or go slightly in the red are not considered very viable. Make your Me Inc. a powerhouse of financial strength.

Since I have been doing this for quite a while now I know full well that the 77% mentioned above are already deciding to skip this financial planning step. Here is why you should power through and create a financial plan:

- It will reduce your general anxiety.
- It will reduce your financial anxiety.
- It can help you overcome financial avoidance and financial rejection behaviors (rejecting the role of money plays in your life).
- It will increase your standard of living if you stick with it a while.
- It will exponentially improve your money performance.

There is a documented link between goal setting and successful life outcomes.[15] There is also a documented link between getting control of your finances and subsequently lowering your stress levels, which creates better physical and mental health.[16] Financial planning is the difference between getting what you need and want, or just living your life without achieving what is important to you.

Financial planning is only associated with retirement planning in our culture. The wealthy, however, understand that financial planning is used to accomplish any goal that requires money and use financial planning daily. In fact, the wealthy spend 10 times more time financial planning than a middle-class person (around ten hours a month).[17] This is why the educational component of the Breakthrough Formula for Prosperity is so vital.

Financial planning, just like wealth building, is a front-loaded task. This means the hardest work is done when you first produce and begin implementing your financial plan. After working with your financial plan for a while, it continues to get easier and easier as time passes. A financial plan is important because it improves your life satisfaction, builds self-esteem, helps you accomplish your goals and builds confidence in abilities to succeed in the future.

Would you like to increase your life satisfaction, your enthusiasm and even your net worth? It starts with increasing your optimism. An optimistic attitude has been linked to wealth creation, goal achievement and a less stressful life. Keep reading to learn the advantages optimism can provide to you.

Chapter 9 Summary Formulas

Lack of Financial Control + Lack of Knowledge =
77% of Americans

Live Paycheck to Paycheck + Ongoing $8,300
Credit Card Debt = 60% of Americans

Financial Denial + Financial Rejection =
Subcategories of Money Avoidance

Financial Goals + Your Financial Data +
Budget + Analyze Budget + Develop Plan +
Take Action = Financial Plan

Reduces Stress + Reduces Anxiety +
Improved Financial Performance +
Improved Health = Benefit of Financial Plan

Total Monthly Income - Total Monthly Expenses =
Monthly Profit or Savings

Chapter 10
From Helplessness to Optimistic Action

Complete the below sentence:

I am most grateful for these three things in my life:

_____

_____

_____

This is the true story of two geological petroleum technicians. Both technicians were employed by the oil and gas industry to take geological samples from the field. The technicians then transported their collected samples back to the petroleum lab for scientific analysis. To do this job, they have to know a great deal about the area they are working in, like geological features and the lay of the land. They also had to know how to navigate the areas safely and understand the best way to take the various soil and rock samples. They had to possess a great deal of knowledge about geology, erosion, plant life and even the general dangers found in the environment in which they worked. These petroleum technicians worked in remote wilderness areas. In this story, our two technicians were taking samples in and around the Big Bend National Park area of Texas.

The first technician always wanted to work in his field. He loved his job and sought this particular job out because he loved working in remote wilderness areas. He enjoyed the local residents around Big Bend, being in the wilderness almost every day and learning about the area's history. He also had an affinity for the plants, birds and animals he encountered in the wilderness. The first technician continually tried to expand his knowledge about the area. Since geological petroleum technicians make a great deal of money, the first technician was able to save and invest his income to create a secure future so he could continue living in the wilderness when he became older.

The second geological petroleum technician did not seek that particular job out. He obtained the job because a friend helped him get into the oil and gas company when he was looking for employment. The second technician believed his job was boring drudgery. He did not particularly enjoy the outdoors and complained about his job regularly to coworkers and family. This technician also made a great deal of money at work. The second technician did like the pay he received, or more accurately he enjoyed spending his pay. He spent his income by first buying a Hummer and then a nice, sporty Porsche. Even though our second technician did not like his job and complained about it often, he made no effort to go anywhere else in the company or to find a different job that he might enjoy more.

As often happens, a round of layoffs came to the oil and gas industry. Both technicians were quickly laid off. The first technician saw the layoff as an opportunity to improve his life. He kept a positive attitude and immediately transitioned himself into being a wilderness guide for visiting tourists in the area he loved so much. He now guides hikers and river explorers and even takes 4X4 journeys with tourists and nature lovers who want to experience the beauty of the back country around Big Bend National Park. He is thrilled to spend every day in a place he loves. Although he does not make as much money as he did when working for the oil and gas industry, he is very happy with his job and is still able to save money.

The second technician had an entirely different perspective. He saw the job loss as a stressful disaster. He complained bitterly about his layoff. He soon saw that his unemployment check was not enough money to cover his expenses. This forced him to get rid of the Porsche first and then the Hummer later because he was not able to keep up with his payments. He finally had to buy a used, economical car to get around.

Additionally, the second technician could not find another job that would pay him anywhere near what he had been making. Job opportunities, he found, are slim in remote areas. So the second technician continued to look for a job and remained unemployed. After a year or so, his unemployment eventually ran out. The second technician still has no job and is still waiting for his oil and gas company to rehire him. Because of this long wait, he is now living on public assistance. He is bitter and unhappy and believes life dealt him a cruel, undeserved blow. He is stressed out over his life situation and has no idea what he will do next other than wait for the gas and oil company (or a competing company) to eventually rehire him.

One of the basic requirements to becoming rich, or even to become reasonably well off financially, is creating and maintaining an optimistic mindset! I am not talking about naive type of optimism where everything is bright and beautiful all the time, even when it is not, nor am I talking about the optimism where you believe everything will just work out and all we have to do is just believe hard enough.

> *This book defines optimism as the inner belief that you have the ability to take control of your life by taking goal-based direct actions. You have the capability and even the obligation to make your future bigger, better and more satisfying to you!*

This is also the type of optimistic mindset that has been scientifically proven to be valuable in both wealth creation and in professional achievement.

If we examine the first technician in the story above, we see that he was more positive than his colleague. He was more resilient and had better life-coping skills. He had gratitude about his life and an appreciation for everything life has provided him. He believed that his own efforts and actions made the difference in improving his circumstances. He fully expects his life to be great, and it is! He has more money and has his financial life under control, which keeps his stress low and his outlook positive. He takes the actions he needs to take to create the future he wants.

According to the website verywellmind.com, the advantages of maintaining a positive attitude include:

- Positive expectations of the future
- Better coping skills when things go wrong
- Ability to persist in your planned course of actions when things go wrong
- Lower stress
- Gratitude for life

- Greater recognition of life's opportunities as they present themselves
- Significantly greater wealth[1]

Goal achievement requires substantial effort up front and a great deal of optimism. You expend effort by taking directed action and defer the gratification of just hanging out or doing other things that you want to do until later. The idea is your efforts today will allow you to do much more of the things you really enjoy in the future. You work to create the desired outcomes that you have decided will make your life better in the future. That means you persist in the face of roadblocks and problems and expend considerable effort to achieve your chosen goals. Deferring gratification requires optimism, like that displayed by the first technician.

> *There are other life advantages for developing an optimistic mindset. During my working career, I noticed pretty quickly that optimists were more popular at work, were liked better by their supervisor and received better work assignments than their negative peers.*

When I noticed this trend, I resolved right then and there to create and maintain a more optimistic attitude. Of course you cannot just flip a switch. Altering my attitude did not just magically happen. It took effort to alter my perceptions, my daily attitude about work and to increase my inner and outward optimism. *(To learn how to develop a long-term positive mindset, see workbook.)*

Scientific research on optimism proved all the advantages I observed regarding my coworkers were accurate. Optimists have better health, better school performance, better work performance, are more popular overall and are elected to public office more often than pessimists.[2] One of the world's foremost experts on optimism is Martin Seligman PhD, (the father of Positive Psychology) who wrote the book, *Learned Optimism: How to Change Your Mind and Your Life* (2nd ed. 2006). Dr. Martin Seligman believes optimism is directly linked to better life outcomes such as a longer life, aging well, and having fewer chronic health problems.[3] His conception of optimism is that when optimists experience setbacks in their plans, they believe the setbacks are temporary and are specific to this particular plan only. When the optimists experience defeat, they typically feel the defeat was not their fault.[4] Optimists believe the future will be bright and are more resilient than pessimists when things inevitably go wrong.

Just as important was Seligman's contrasting concept of the attitude of pessimism. His theory is that pessimists believe that bad events in life will impact them for a long time and will threaten everything they have done.[5] Not surprisingly, pessimists give up and quit more frequently because they believe nothing they do will change their eventual defeat—even though defeat could well be temporary with corrective strategies. Pessimists lack the resilience to keep trying in the face of setbacks and view even moderate problems as insurmountable.

Seligman also linked the concept of pessimism to learned helplessness. Learned helplessness is an important concept in both psychology and in finance. It is the idea that nothing you do will make any difference in solving your problem(s). It was first explored back in the 60s and 70s by Dr. Seligman and Steven Maier in laboratory experiments where dogs were subjected to shocks at regular intervals.[6] There were three groups of dogs. A group who was not shocked, a group who learned to avoid the shock by leaping into another chamber inside their kennels and a group that had no way to avoid the pending shock.[7]

All three groups were then put in a second experiment that was similar. In this experiment, all three groups were placed in a box with a low barrier they could easily clear to avoid a pending shock. Those that learned they could avoid a coming shock by entering a different chamber of the box and those who were not shocked previously would leap over the low barrier to avoid a shock if they had an opportunity to do so. However, those who previously had no way to escape a coming shock did not even try to do so—this phenomenon was dubbed "learned helplessness."[8]

To show the relevance to humans, Dr. Seligman did a similar experiment with two groups of people. The first group was placed in a room where loud and unpleasant sounds were being played. The first group could stop the loud and unpleasant noises by pulling a lever down. The second group in the room could not stop the noise and the lever did nothing to stop it. On the second round, everyone had the ability to stop the noise by pulling a lever down. In the second round, the first group that were not able to stop the loud noises in their first round did not even try to do so during their second round. This group exhibited the same symptoms of learned helplessness the dogs had displayed.[9]

Learned helplessness can negatively impact your day-to-day finances and life outcomes. Learned helplessness stems from early family experiences. It is believed it can be created by a mother or other caregiver who passes her learned helpless frame of reference on to her offspring. It has also been seen sometimes in children raised in institutions where they have no control over their lives.[10] It may also be caused by abuse a child cannot escape or by being severely neglected.[11] These types of upbringings sometimes create a learned helplessness world view, but that does not mean that this type of upbringing will always cause these problems or these symptoms. As the ACE study demonstrated, it also depends upon the child and his or her support system.

> *All of these concepts and how they impact us are important because learned helplessness is associated with higher rates of depression, anxiety, lack of financial resources and a lack of resilience.*[12]

Would you like to significantly increase your optimism? Can you imagine how great it would be to remain more optimistic when overcoming your problems to reduce stress and to even increase your income? The Breakthrough Formula for Prosperity shows us the best way to retrain our brains to be more optimistic. We begin by modifying the self-defeating lessons we learned from our past. Reframing our view of the past will improve all aspects of our life. We then educate ourselves about what we need to know to move forward, and then we set goals and push toward the results we desire. To accomplish this goal, we will again employ the effective technique of optimistic reframing.

As in other chapters, we begin by reframing the messages we learned when we were young. In addition to reframing our past, we can also reframe our current challenges and problems. Optimistic reframing is about changing our thoughts and feelings to create a more positive and confident story. This will reduce our stress and lower unhelpful feelings that enter our minds. Once we have lowered our stress level, we can think more clearly and more creatively. If you were laid off, for example, telling yourself a positive story about this event rather than becoming depressed or down about your situation creates better outcomes. So rather than telling yourself and others you were laid off you might say you are in a career transition. Other positive reframes in this scenario include:

- Exploration of better opportunities during a temporary break from work
- Repackaging your many skills to improve your employment situation
- Training to upgrade your skills

As we recall from past chapters, we don't always consciously understand what lessons we have learned from our past. It is difficult sometimes to recognize our subconscious self-defeating beliefs that drive our less helpful behaviors. We can begin to notice these messages by being mindful and monitoring our thoughts and feelings. Negative or exaggerated pessimistic beliefs and thoughts need to be immediately reframed into something more positive.[13] This is a life-long challenge I continue to work on every day.

In every situation, there are aspects we have control over. Using the oil and gas technician story as an example, the technicians certainly could not control that they were laid off from their jobs. They could control, however, how they prepared their lives in the event of a layoff. We can't control job security during certain stages of our economic cycle, but we can control where we live or the skills we have to market in the areas that we live. In most situations, taking charge of the things you can control will almost immediately reduce your stress and improve your outlook.[14]

It takes a little practice to see the opportunities presented by problems that block your progress. The more you practice this skill, the better you become in using it.[15] If you are not naturally positive, being positive can be difficult. It is really easy and takes no particular skill or talent to be negative. Thinking optimistically, however, takes more mental effort and practice. Optimism is directly linked with the expectation of a brighter future, which is a necessary element to having the energy to achieve your chosen objectives. Without an expectation of a bright future, you are not willing to put in the work needed to overcome the inevitable problems that will block your path.[16] Without optimism, we would never try anything new or be willing to stretch to reach our goals. Those without optimism rarely take risks!

To bring this all together, we now need to look at the workplace. This is the place where achievement matters, is recorded and is sought continually. Work is a great place to examine how people achieve their goals. Every workplace function can and is broken down into performance goals. Usually, these are profit goals. In the case of government, they are nonprofit or outcome-directed goals.

> The workplace values employees who display a high level of optimism, self-efficacy, intrinsic motivation and perseverance. These optimists are the people who blaze the trails needed to achieve the organization's goals.[17]

These folks display a high level of commitment to their work because they believe in their employers or because of an internal work ethic (intrinsic motivation). No matter what happens, these people can be counted upon to achieve their agreed-upon goals—assuming it can be done. Sometimes, optimistic people even achieve their goals when it seemed impossible to others that they could do so.

Future-centered activities (like wealth building, goal achievement and planning) are related to optimism. Optimism can also be directly linked to increased resilience, persisting in the face of inevitable difficulties and the ability to defer gratification, which is a skill needed to build wealth and achieve goals.

Do you ever feel trapped inside your own life or feel bored and numb to your daily experiences? Do you wonder what the meaning of it all is? Do you spend money because you are unhappy with your life? If so, keep reading to learn about creating a life's purpose to increase your life's meaning and satisfaction.

Chapter 10 Summary Formulas

Resilience + Expectation of a Bright Future + Happier + Better Personal Relationships = Optimistic Attitude

Learned Helplessness + Depression + Anxiety + Easily Giving Up + Unhappiness + Poor Financial Control = Pessimism

Self-Worth + Belief That What You Do Makes a Difference + Belief That You Can Adequately Handle Problems = Self-Efficacy

Optimism + Self-Efficacy + Intrinsic Motivation = Goal Achievement Success

Chapter 11
From Going With The Flow to Pursuing a Life's Purpose

Answer the question and complete the sentence below.

What are your most important values?

_____

_____

_____

_____

Based on my values, _____ is my life purpose.

I have been lucky in so many different ways. From the age of about 16 on, I have been on a purposeful, directed mission to save the world! I understand that I am not likely to do it in a big, adventure movie way.

My first career was providing safety, security and a modicum of justice through the police services I provided to my community. I took this mission very seriously and worked at it diligently for over thirty years. I was very successful and proud of my work there. Now, I am doing my bit to save the world by teaching people how to create financial prosperity in their lives. I do this by writing, coaching and personally instructing on money management and success topics. Both of these life purposes are vitally important, and I have found fulfillment in pursuing each of them.

What is your life purpose? Luckily, there are an infinite number of problems and improvements that require our personal attention and direct action. Take the famous parable of the boy who strolled along the beach early each morning throwing starfish back into the ocean so they didn't bake and die when the sun came out. A man saw the boy throwing the starfish back into the ocean and asked him, "Why do you do that? It doesn't make a difference. The boy threw a starfish in and replied, "Well, it makes a difference to that one!" then happily continued walking along the beach throwing starfish back into the ocean.

Not having a life purpose leaves you rudderless and going with the flow. I did have a brief period where I got lost in the fog of life and veered off track from my life purpose. Shortly after high school, I got a job at the General Motors assembly plant. This was not what I had planned for my life, but I wasn't quite old enough to join the police department, and I was attending college part time. This job opportunity felt too good to turn down, so I took it. The job paid extremely well, it had great benefits and I was treated very well at work most of the time. After working at the job a few years, I absolutely hated it. I felt it was entirely unfulfilling and I was serving no purpose. I now fully recognize that this was my issue and was never my employer's problem.

To me, the job felt like the punishment of Sisyphus from Greek mythology who was condemned by the God Zeus to push a giant bolder up a hill every day. Once at the top, it would roll back down, and Sisyphus had to start pushing the rock all over again.

Although some writers theorize Sisyphus eventually accepted his fate and found fulfillment in his eternal task, I certainly never did with my assembly line job!

One day I was leaving work and a thought suddenly popped into my brain. *Well, here is another day of my life wasted.* That realization alarmed me. I knew I had to get back on track with my life purpose and my goals. My last day at General Motors, about six months later, was a happy day for me. Very likely, General Motors was happy to be rid of me as well.

In this book, we define life purpose as our central motivation or primary concern in life. A life purpose is supported by your most important values, and serving your life purpose gives you the motivation you need to get up every day and accomplish the goals that are important to you. It guides your decisions about life, your finances and your day-to-day actions. Not having a purpose can leave you feeling lost, bored, unsatisfied and generally unhappy. Your life lacks the meaning or context your brain craves.

Do you ever feel trapped inside your own life? Do you ever spend money because you are unhappy and need relief from the monumental stress you face? If so, look once again to our Breakthrough Formula for Prosperity to show you how to create a better reality. To improve our finances, we must first improve our lives. An excellent way to significantly improve your life is by selecting and pursuing a life purpose. After selecting your purpose, you set goals that serve that purpose, then you educate yourself with the knowledge you need to help yourself and others.

> *You have the total freedom and even the obligation to choose a life purpose that fulfills you!*

It can be whatever you decide! If you have no idea what your life purpose should be, no worries at all. Just peruse the quotes in the workbook section of Chapter 11 about beauty, freedom, passion or serving mankind, and pick one of those if you'd rather. What really matters is that your life purpose is positive in nature and excites you. You can double its benefit to your life if you serve others while pursuing it.[1]

Why commit to a life purpose? Committing fully to a cause larger than yourself ignites your passion and provides your life with greater context and meaning. Your life purpose should support your most important values in life.[2] This is not only important for mankind but equally important for your own psychological, physical and financial well-being.

A goal and a life purpose are slightly different. For example, let's assume you decide your life purpose is to assure the U.S. has the cleanest beaches of any place in the world. In regard to your life purpose, your goal might then be to start a nonprofit organization that cleans up beaches and politically advocates for cleaner beaches. Now, what should your financial goal be? It would be helpful, you decide, to not have to work at a job while you fulfill your purpose so you can devote all your time to this cause. So your financial goal needs to be that you become financially independent. Or you might decide that you need to grow your organization to be large enough to pay yourself a salary so you can devote all of your time to this cause without waiting until you build enough money to become financially independent. This is how your life purpose and your goals work together.

Your purpose can be found in your current career or could be something entirely separate from your job.

For example, during my police career, my life purpose was to provide the best police service possible in order to improve the community. I was entirely dedicated to this, and most of my goals were focused on achieving that one mission. Later, when I retired, I was done with that life purpose and shifted my focus. My new life purpose was to improve the dismal financial literacy levels in the U.S. I wanted to help others become as prosperous as I have become. I started to shift my life purpose several years before I retired, so it was a relatively smooth transition. Your life purpose can change, and that is okay. If it doesn't fulfill you, you can change it without penalty.

If you have a small, private business, your life purpose can be to provide the best service or value possible to your customers. If you work at a retail store, it could be to provide the best customer service or service with a smile to brighten customers' days. Maybe your purpose is something you do in your spare time, like helping people in your community learn to read. These life purposes provide you with a sense of fulfillment no other endeavors can possibly match in the long run. In fact, it has been shown that a purposeful path leads to better mental health and a happier, more uplifting life experience.[3] Study after study has shown that humans need (maybe even require) a life purpose. Those who pursue a purpose have fewer life problems.

A purposeful life provides us an opportunity to mentally step outside of ourselves.[4] Dramatic improvements in attitude, loneliness, depression and health have been found to be encompassed within the pursuit (not necessarily the achievement) of a life purpose.[5] Having a life purpose has even been shown to help reduce substance abuse problems in drug and alcohol addicts.[6] Humans seem to require a life purpose to function at our best.

Study after study also finds that pursuing a life purpose leads to greater financial prosperity.

> For example, a 2016 study proved those who lived and pursued their life purpose made more money. This remained consistent over time (as measured by the study participant's net worth). This was true even when the study was adjusted for race, sex and financial background.[7]

It is believed the pursuit of a life purpose over a long period of time strengthens the ability to push through problems to achieve your goals and help us achieve our long-term goals more consistently.[8] Long-term goals are achieved by increasing your ability to defer gratification, which is an essential primary ability needed to be successful in many aspects of life—particularly financial prosperity.[9]

Only 25% of Americans report having a clear sense of purpose in life.[10] So 75% of Americans are missing this opportunity to improve their mental and physical health, life satisfaction and their finances.

Chapter 11 Summary Formulas

Life Purpose = Improved Mental Health + Physical Health + Higher Net Worth + Longer and Happier life

Chapter 12
From Indecision to Financial Confidence

Complete the below sentence:

On a scale of 1 to 10, with 10 being the highest confidence, I rate myself at _____ for making day-to-day financial decisions.

My friend Mark called me to tell me about his great luck and fortune. Mark's family just sold his parents' home and farmland in southern Ohio. He and his siblings inherited this farm from his deceased parents. He received around $350,000 as his share of the sale of the family's land and home. He asked me what he should do with this money. I briefly explained investing to him and suggested mutual index funds with low fees that are very important to a long-term investor. I told him 350k might grow into well over a million dollars in financial assets in 20 to 30 years, , and it would require very little effort on his part.

Mark was clearly overwhelmed by our conversation. I explained to him that investing was not complicated, and that I could easily teach him what he needed to know. Then he began talking about a fear of losing his money in the stock market. I told him the longer he was invested, the less chance he would lose money and that his money could likely triple or quadruple based on the return on investment he earned over time. When he continued to express doubt that he could manage his investments, I told him I could give an investment advisor's name that I trusted to make sure he had investments that made sense. Although having an investment advisor is not my first choice, it is always much better than doing nothing.

Can you guess what my friend Mark did? If you guessed nothing, then you would be correct! Instead, he punted the problem. Eventually, he bought big-ticket items with his money — a boat, a new truck to pull his new boat and numerous other big-boy toys. I wish I could say this was an unusual occurrence, but this story is very much the norm. Much of our culture is focused on spending money.[1] This is what they grew up doing every day. Nearly 60% of middle-class earners claim they are broke, and nearly 20% of high earners (150k or more annually) say they are broke.[2]

Since spending is what we know and routinely do, when the choices are foreign or seem daunting, spending money becomes the default.

When indecision impacts your financial decisions, you revert to the stories and lessons about money you were taught growing up, such as spending money to have "the good life." This is why indecision is very harmful to your financial future. Without an understanding of what you want to accomplish and the means and methods you will utilize to get the job done, you revert back to the lessons and messages that are your financial default, such as the practice of spending.

To clarify what I mean, consider that the millennial generation's top complaints to their therapists are feelings of intense pressure to succeed financially and professionally. Additionally, they feel overwhelmed by their finances and have decision fatigue from trying to make the many needed financial decisions they must make.[3] Without a solid knowledge base to draw upon, indecision reigns supreme.

The Breakthrough Formula for Prosperity can help us with financial indecision, or a lack of financial confidence, by showing us how to overcome this very common problem:

1. Create more financial confidence through education.
2. Improve our life and finances by reframing our incorrect money scripts fostered upon us by society at large.
3. Set goals to positively improve our financial confidence and life.

Did you also know that financial indecision costs you money? Usually, the cost is losing opportunities to indecision. In the investing world, losing money by doing nothing or taking a less profitable action is called "opportunity costs." It is the difference between what you have now as a result of your decision or spending and what you could have had with a different (usually better) choice.

Take the decision to purchase a boat for 50k over the alternative of investing the same amount of money. You not only lose the money you spent on your boat, but you also lose the money your boat purchase could have produced for you over a set time period in various investments.

For example, if you earned 5% annually on 50k, after a year, that would be a $52,500 difference between your decision to buy a boat vs. investing that same amount of money. Then add in the cost of the boat maintenance, licensing and operation. Each year, the cost differences between these two money choices grows further and further apart as the investment could have grown in your accounts. After five years, the initial 50k could have earned $14,168 in interest income alone *(see workbook for other examples)*.

Indecision also costs you time — the time you spend ruminating for hours trying to make the perfect decision, the time it takes to fix any messes you created from your indecision and the lost opportunity costs. Conversely, the decision to invest (typically) makes you money and generates income rather than costing you anything. Also, the longer you are invested in the stock market, the greater the chance you will make money and the less risky this choice (investing in stocks) becomes.

Confidence in your own financial ability and decisiveness makes all the difference in your financial outcomes.

- Financial Consumer Agency of Canada has shown a link between financial knowledge and improved financial capabilities.[4]
- *The Journal of Economic Psychology* demonstrated that financial confidence leads to greater wealth.[5]
- A University of British Columbia study demonstrated that people with more financial resources have greater peace of mind.[6]
- Northwestern Mutual discovered a clear link between those with higher financial confidence having greater life satisfaction and happiness.[7]

I knew very little about finances in the beginning. I gained financial knowledge and confidence by:

1. Reading personal finance books
2. Subscribing to financial newsletters
3. Listening to financial podcasts

As we have learned from the Breakthrough Formula for Prosperity, we also need to reframe our incorrect, inner money scripts. See these examples of false money stories and improved reframes:

- False story, "Spend money to enjoy the good life."

   Living in debt misery is not now, nor has ever been, the "good life." Reframe your story to "I have now learned to defer my wants until later when I have more financial resources to buy the things I want without going into significant debt."
- False story, "I don't deserve to be happy."

   You and everyone else on earth deserves to be as happy as you can manage to be. Reframe this ineffective and false story to, "I, like everyone else, deserve to be happy with my life and myself."
- False story, "I don't know anything about money."

   You might not know much about money because you have not yet been taught about it. Reframe this inaccurate story to a more accurate one. "I am learning about money to create a more prosperous and satisfying life."
- False story, "Money is way too complicated a subject for me to learn about!"

I know many people of average intelligence who managed to get rich. It is not that difficult to learn. It is just a skill you decide you need and then go out and obtain. It is like riding a bicycle, learning to change your car's flat tire or a certification at work. Reframe your money story to, "I've got this!"

If your finances are disaster right now, don't worry. You can accomplish all your long-term financial goals with just a little more focused effort. You can clean up your finances and move forward. The idea is you start at the bottom (short term) and work your way upward (long term) toward your larger goal.

1. Create a financial plan and its accompanying budget.
2. Reduce your daily, weekly then monthly spending.
3. Increase your income.
4. Reduce your debt and improve credit.
5. Create an emergency fund.
6. Start investing your savings.
7. Create a large group of financial assets that will fund your future life.

In previous chapters we learned that focusing our larger financial and life goals helps us resist spending temptations. That fact is very relevant here. Focusing on your long-term goals will keep you moving toward your goalposts.

Did you know your past money story can negatively impact how much your employer pays you today? Did you know that how you think also impacts your income? As strange as this may seem, it is absolutely true. If you want to learn more, then read the next chapter on creating income.

Chapter 12 Summary Formulas

Goal Setting + Income Creation + Budgeting + Savings + Investing = Prosperity

Chapter 13
From Culturally Restricted Thinking to a Growth Mindset

Answer the following questions.

What values did I inherit that help me succeed financially?

_____

Which values did I inherit that inhibit financial thinking?

_____

Most working-class Americans do not typically become rich. Benjamin Franklin was a notable exception to this rule. He was one of the few founding fathers who created a great deal of wealth in his life. Most of the founders, like Thomas Jefferson for example, ended up passing away with very little financial means. Although Benjamin Franklin created enough wealth to become financially independent at the early age of 42, he started his working career at 15. He came from a large family that lived in near poverty. Young Benjamin began his working life as an apprentice to his brother who owned and operated a print shop. Benjamin's brother was extremely jealous of Ben's obvious intellect and business abilities. He kept Ben on a short leash to prevent him from excelling.

Ben eventually raised money from some friends, illegally fled his brother's apprenticeship and set up his own printing shop in another state where his brother had no hold over him. Ben's print shop soon became hugely successful. Of course, Ben had boundless energy and zeal and started many related side businesses. The point of creating these various side businesses is that each new business brought in additional streams of income. His side jobs included:

- Author
- Book publisher
- Paper mill/production
- Printing supplies sales and paper production
- A wholesale paper delivery business (to deliver his paper and others)
- Postmaster (salary from his appointment)

All of these income streams, plus his many business investments, made Benjamin Franklin quite wealthy.[1]

> Ben Franklin was not only a founding father of our country, he also developed the first franchising system used in the Colonies around the year 1731. He used his system to become the wealthiest person in America.[2]

His franchising system appeared to be structured as a partnership with a licensing agreement. In addition to the franchisee purchasing the Franklin license, it obligated the franchisee to purchase all their printing supplies from Franklin and to publish Franklin's written material—such as his *Poor Richard Almanac*. He expanded this system throughout the Colonies that created dozens and dozens of various revenue streams.

You may have never learned that multiple-income stream creation could make you more financially secure or even rich. You may have learned this when you grew older from financial literature, but chances are very good that your family did not teach you this lesson growing up. Instead, you were always taught to get an "education and get a good job!"

These days, creating multiple income streams is actually a common practice, but it is not a new concept. It was a common practice in ancient times by merchants who traveled the trade routes to create and sustain wealth.

Financially successful people commonly use this method. Consider the study reported in the business publication *Inc.* that determined that three income streams seems to be the break-through point for creating wealth (with the very rich creating even more income streams).

- 65% of millionaires had at least three income streams.
- 29% of millionaires had five or more streams of income.[3]

If you want to be wealthy or financially secure, you should know that the more income streams you can create, the more freedom you can build into your life. Here are some examples of additional income streams:

A. Income from your regular job
B. Income from a side hustle (side job)
C. Income from your investment portfolio
D. Income from a pension
E. Income from disability payments if you are disabled
F. Income from a business you created
G. Income from your hobbies

H. Income from rental properties
I. Income from social security
J. Income from military service or military reserves
K. Income from a military pension
L. Income from additional sources not mentioned here

If you have a spouse, he or she should also create multiple income streams. When you add all of your income streams together, it becomes a powerful and resilient flow of financial support into your life.

Multiple income streams provide more financial security than any single "good job" could ever bestow. Plus, secure, "good jobs" are now pretty much a thing of the past. As soon as a company faces revenue loss from an economic downturn, they immediately begin cutting their payroll. This is also true even in the government, when tax revenue shrinks from a retracting economy.

Something that holds people back from financial success is the culturally shared concept of financial scarcity, where the majority of people in a community believe few financial resources are available for them, and they must work hard to obtain what they get. When this is considered the norm by an entire class, it is called socioeconomic scarcity.[4] As you recall from the previous chapters, those without the needed financial resources have significantly lowered cognition, a narrowed focus on the immediate and impaired ability to make correct decisions.[5]

If we inventory our cultural beliefs, how many of the below values or practices are familiar to you?

· Get an education, get a good job and then save money for retirement.

- You have to scrape and fight for every dime.
- You must work very hard to become wealthy.
- You should strive to be comfortable, because your chances of being rich are slim.
- Money is in short supply.
- I had rather be happy than rich.
- The way to make money is to have a J-O-B.
- Ambition is crass and unseemly.
- Starting your own business is very risky.[6]

We learned from the Breakthrough Formula for Prosperity the importance of correcting the dysfunctional, subconscious lessons and beliefs we developed from our childhood experiences. Along with those past lessons and subconscious beliefs, we also inherited an array of values and practices from our particular culture or subculture growing up. We can correct our inaccurate beliefs with financial education. Without the education component of the Breakthrough Formula for Prosperity, we are stuck trying to create wealth using incorrect beliefs and practices.

How many of your peers from grade school or high school became wealthy. How many wealthy people do you know? Unfortunately, there is no major movement to help middle-class and low-income families learn about finances, so our money practices rarely lead to significant wealth. Not understanding finances leads to phrases and thinking such as, "The rich get richer," or "It takes money to make money." This is where financial education plays a critical role in changing our financial practices.

It would be helpful to adopt a growth mindset. A growth mindset is knowing your skills and abilities can easily be enhanced through education, effort and by learning new skills. You understand there will be failures along the way, but don't fear inevitable failures. With a growth mindset, you understand the power of leading a purposeful life and relentlessly pursuing your long-term goals. A person with a growth mindset never doubts they will be rich.[7]

Within the context of financial literacy, maintain an open mind and consider reframing your past cultural values and practices into a more effective growth mindset. Consider the following reframed, contrasting attitudes of the wealthy in relation to the above list of common middle-class values and money practices:

- Some of the most financially and professionally successful people in the world do not have a formal degree. A degree certainly doesn't hurt (unless you are deeply in debt for it), but in no way will it guarantee any kind of success. Knowledge, not education is the key to earning.
- In today's economy, jobs are always changing, so a "secure job" is nonexistent.
- Don't worry about retirement so much as creating a high net worth. Create wealth, and your retirement will naturally take care of itself. Plus, even the wealthy don't necessarily retire if they find new passions or financial endeavors.
- You can be rich if that is your goal and, just as importantly, if you are willing to work the steps needed to create that outcome in your life.
- There is no scarcity of money! The government runs machines that print this stuff 24 hours a day, seven days a week.

Money scarcity is a flawed mindset. Wealth exists for those who put in the effort and thought to go out and obtain it.

· The wealthy don't focus on working hard. Instead, they focus on working smart. With a few exceptions requiring technical skills, you can make more money by *thinking* than you ever could by being paid for your labor.

· We do require income, but we do not necessarily have to have a formal job to create that income. Here are common ways to generate income that don't involve traditional labor:

  › Produce a product and sell it to a company.

  › Produce designs and sell them (fashion, T-shirts, etc.).

  › Write and publish e-books.

  › Income from investments, like dividends

  › Income such as rent from real estate you own

  › Reselling items you purchased (from land to household items) or control items through leverage—like purchase options

· There are many different ways to generate income. You are limited only by your imagination. *For additional examples see workbook.*

· You can be both rich and happy—I certainly am. Being only one or the other is a false narrative. Take it from me, the two are not mutually exclusive.

· Ambition is neither bad nor crass unless you do bad or unethical things to further your ambition. Poor ethics create needless, excessive risks and heartache for everyone. Those who lack ethics eventually have poor outcomes. Without ambition, however, you would never likely make a high salary or create wealth without an extreme desire to do so.

- Starting a business (depending on the business) is no more risky than most jobs in terms of longevity—especially given our modern economy. Starting a business remains one of the fastest ways to produce significant wealth.

Now let's take this concept a step further. In previous chapters, we learned that our self-worth impacts our finances. We learned that our self-esteem also impacts every aspect of our lives including what job we have, our romantic relationships and even our day-to-day life satisfaction. Did you know that self-worth is also directly related to your income? Study after study has shown a direct link between a person's inner feelings of value (and being valued by an organization) with the amount of income they earn annually.[8] How does one impact the other?

> At work, when you think about your performance, do you think mostly about your past successes or your failures?

Those with lower self-esteem recall stories at work that had poor outcomes. These are their go-to thoughts when they consider their value within an organization. So naturally they act in a congruent manner since they expect similar outcomes in their future. The opposite is true of high earners. They look back to their positive accomplishments and expect nothing less for their future. Those with high self-esteem are confident, outgoing and act in a congruent manner. This inspires inner and outer confidence in their employees and/or peers and creates success.[9]

One way to make more money is to improve your feelings of self-worth and confidence. Not only will it increase your income level but, as the Breakthrough Formula for Prosperity has shown us, it will also improve every other aspect of your life!

A study published in the *British Psychology Journal* attempted to determine if this process could be reversed. Could a person's work performance and self-esteem improve by giving him or her a pay raise (to raise self-esteem and performance)? After controlling for organization tenure and previous raises the study did find evidence this approach is valid. Performance improvement did occur with a salary raise.[10]

Here is one final thought about income and the socioeconomic class values that hold you back from financial success.

A high net worth can actually save your life!

If you get sick or seriously injured, will you have the financial resources you require to get the type of medical care you need? The more serious your illness, the more this matters and the harder it becomes for you. Those with less financial resources face significant hurdles in this area. Arguments about healthcare equity aside, not only do poorer people have less money to pay for their immediate medical needs, those who have jobs with less income also face the reality of dealing with lower health coverage benefits. A new study now shows those people who have a higher income have a lower mortality rate than those who have fewer financial resources.[11] Not only that, but those who had a higher income lived longer and had more years of healthier life than those with less income.[12] So much for the "I'd rather be happy than rich" crowd!

We all must face and deal with our limitations or disabilities, but we shouldn't let them scare or deter us. After all, we all carry our heavy packs upon our back, but we are also born with our own unique personal talents, abilities, knowledge and varied interests. You are unique and special! Honor your talents by utilizing your abilities. Maximize your skills and talents with a growth mindset.

Do you want to make the most of your income? Then you need to know how to conquer your budget. What's that? You absolutely hate budgeting? Well, me too! Keep reading to learn how to make peace with it.

Chapter 13 Summary Formulas

Income Stream + Income Stream + Income Stream + Even More Income Streams = Wealth

Growth Mindset + Reframed Middle-Class Mindset = Wealth

Chapter 14
From Budget Avoidance to Budget Mastery

Answer the following question.

Would you rather create and follow a budget or hit your finger fairly hard with a hammer?

D o you choose budget or hammer? If you hate (or even fear) budgeting enough that you would rather smash your finger with a hammer than create and follow a budget you are not alone. I did an informal survey of friends on social media, and 30% of those who responded chose hammer over following a budget.

During the time I was single, my stated goal (said out loud and frequently) was to do as little work as possible on my day-to-day finances. I was not horrible with my finances, but I detested spending the time needed to maintain a weekly or even monthly budget. My tendency was to neglect all of these financial chores whenever I possibly could.

That being said, I also had financial and wealth-related goals, and I wasn't about to sacrifice my goals or give up on them. So, to keep my financial chore list as small as possible, I used automatic payments that came out of my checking account each month for most of my bills. I made sure the money for these payments would always be there. I kept my monthly check writing as low as I possibly could.

I also did some very financially smart things during this time period as well. I had small amounts of money from my paycheck automatically sent to my savings account, so it required zero effort on my part. I also sent a small amount to a vacation savings account. I kept all my debts low (partly because extra debt would mean I would have to track more finances). With the money left over from my biweekly paychecks, I bought gas, food, and any extras with cash.

If I splurged somewhere along the way, sometimes I would be eating peanut butter and jelly or canned tuna until my next payday. Other times, I only had enough gas to get to work and back. I can remember being invited to someone's house for a home-cooked meal (yes please!), but I had to decline because I didn't have enough gas money to get there. I had to save what I had to get back and forth to work.

I also routed as much money as I could to my 401(k) (work-sponsored investing account) straight from my paychecks. I increased that amount at least annually if not more often. Later, Robert Kiyosaki would popularize the technique of routing money to savings and investing accounts before paying bills, as "Pay Yourself First."[1] All the while, I just thought I was being lazy. I didn't realize I was on the cutting edge of wealth building! This kept me out of any major trouble while always increasing my net worth via my investment accounts. Luckily, I loved investing, so I was happy to complete that task.

I will say that my budget avoidance was only a general rule.

When the going got tough, however, I would abandon my laissez-fare budgeting style and step up to accomplish whatever I had to do. A couple times in my life I created a crisis budget, which is an entirely different animal from your day-to-day budget (explained in next chapter later in this chapter and in workbook).

My wife, Lisa, has a very analytical personality. When I married her, I knew there would be changes. She soon put a stop to my nonsense and took control over our joint budgets, paychecks and checking accounts. She worked the numbers down to the penny. That certainly doesn't mean everything always came in at the end of month as budgeted—after all, we had three kids between us—but our family budget was dramatically different from my single-guy budget. Just by improving our budget management practices, she increased our savings each month. More savings led to even more investing. We always made sure to pay ourselves first. Her budget was very goal directed, and the budget listed our progress toward our goals front and center.

Our shared financial goal was to create freedom by becoming financially independent. This overriding goal was very important to us. The fact that our goals aligned was not an accident. After two previous divorces (for both of us) we made sure our goals were congruent before we became serious about our relationship together and frequently reinforced our goals with each other by discussing them at length. In fact, whenever we would consider a large purchase (new car, hot tub, boat or anything else nonessential), we would discuss how this impacted our goals. This was a great technique that kept us mostly on track and with low debt.

In previous chapters we discussed people who feel totally lost when dealing with their finances. One would think that most people would gladly use budgeting as a tool to gain control over their money. Sadly, surveys consistently show a range of only 33% to 38% are willing to take the time and expend the effort needed to create and follow through on a budget.[2]

Three primary reasons people detest budgeting:

1. According to psychologist Brad Klontz, the word budget implies to our brain that a famine is coming. All we can do is think about what we will no longer have.[3] Our brains believe that we are losing our resources, fun, happiness, good times and life enjoyment will become a thing of the past. Deprivation, loss, and hard times have now come upon us, and we will suffer.

2. We have all set up budgets in the past that felt arduous and restrictive, and we gave up; or, we used up all our willpower to resist temptations.[4] We ended up slipping and buying things we wanted to feel better about our lives. There went the budget!

3. Budgets make us feel very anxious.[5] You have to face the sum total of all your previous actions. Your past comes home to roost, so to speak, right on the piece of paper or computer spreadsheet in front of your face. Then we have to develop a plan to deal with the financial issues we've created for ourselves. This can be anxiety-inducing for anyone.

Applying the Breakthrough Formula for Prosperity shows us how to overcome these issues, or at least gives us a fighting chance at doing so. We utilize all elements of the Breakthrough Formula to overcome our budgeting roadblocks, and we have to start by reframing our feelings about our budget(s) to reduce the emotions our budgets create. As stated in previous chapters, subconscious emotions create feelings and actions that sabotage our financial efforts. We will also use goal-directed actions to move us forward. Finally, we will become financially educated about the most effective method of thinking and utilizing a budget to support our goals and dreams.

Element 1. The Reframe Component:

Brad Klontz suggests reframing and replacing the term budget with "spending plan." Your brain does not associate a spending plan with the hardships and stress of a budget. A spending plan is essentially what I used during my single years. I automated everything I possibly could and had a plan outlining how I was going to spend what was left over.[6] That didn't mean every penny went exactly where it was expected to go, but it provided me an outline for what to do with my money.

Klontz also suggests that your spending plan should always put the focus on achieving your goals. Focusing on your goals keeps you motivated and on track.[7] For example, the budget my wife Lisa creates for us always lists our goals and progress toward those goals as the most prominent feature in our budget document in big, bold letters.

Element 2. The Education Component:

As mentioned above, using willpower to avoid spending tends to drain us. Once we blow our budget, many times we never bother going back to it. The problem we face is that we only have so much willpower, and we can (temporarily) use it all up. Once we have exhausted our reserves, we end up engaging in spending that blows up our hard-won progress. Research has shown there are strategies we can use to increase our success.

- Avoid situations that cause you to spend money. Stay out of stores, malls and off Amazon unless you must go there.
- Remind yourself that you have decided to reward yourself later rather than spend money now. Be sure to build small rewards into your budget for following it.
- Use the distraction technique. Every time you think about spending, decide to think about your goals instead. This technique, although seemingly very simplistic, has been proven to work extremely well.[8]

People feel anxious about budgets because a budget will likely tell you things you would rather not know—like you are spending more money than you are bringing in. This can create feelings of shame and guilt surrounding your finances. We've talked about shame and guilt in previous chapters and good ways to overcome them. Just remember, you are more than your net worth! You are certainly more than your financial history. Also, a budget at the end of the day is just a plan. In fact, your budget is entirely your own plan.

Element 3. The Goals Component:

You have the power and ability to change your financial situation. You have the ability to control life outcomes and create an entirely new reality that begins solely within your own mind. This incredible power flows from your ability to:

1. Visualize a new future.
2. Create written goals to achieve your vision.
3. Make a plan of action to create your new vision.
4. Take action to achieve that reality.
5. Track progress and celebrate your victories.

However, to create your new world order, you must first understand your current information. The first order of business is to figure out how much you are spending. Track every dime you spend for a couple months. That will ease you into the process and help you begin to get a better picture of where your money is going. As a side note, recording your spending moves all spending into your conscious brain and eliminates subconscious spending. When you become more aware of your spending, you will find that it naturally decreases.

In its simplest form, a budget simply records income and expenses. The ultimate goal of a budget is to allow us to analyze income and expense information and determine where our money is going. Using that information provides us with the ability to make decisions about our daily activities and which of those activities are important in our lives and which ones are expendable or changeable to save money. This process is how we not only gain control of our money, but actually gain control over our lives.

The budget I prefer to teach is the 50/30/20 budget. This budget concentrates on net pay—a paycheck after payroll taxes are deducted (as opposed to gross which is before the payroll taxes are deducted). The broad categories and ideal percentages for budget are as follows:

1. 50% for regular monthly bills
2. 30% for wants
3. 20% for savings

Maybe you can't hit these percentages in these various categories at this moment. After all, not many people are saving 20% of their pay these days.

In the spending plan I used as a single person, I took 30% in cash from my paycheck and spent as I saw fit until my next payday. That move helped provide me with the freedom I needed, so my lifestyle did not feel quite so restricted. The 50% in bills and 20% in savings were both automated and required little to no effort on my part.

A budget can run for a day, a week, monthly or even quarterly. My lovely wife will even do an annual budget with budget projections—just like a business. This doesn't mean we can't deviate, but at least we have a general roadmap where we are headed. In fact, if you are anxious about creating and following a budget, ease into budgeting. What if you did a budget for a single day, then a week and eventually created a monthly budget? This technique allows you to desensitize yourself to budget anxiety or fear.[9]

If your anxiety is still too great about creating a spending plan, a good strategy is to obtain a budget buddy! Have someone work with you. This can be a trusted friend or an actual financial coach you hire. A budget coach can help provide you with the emotional support you need. A coach or budget buddy can also help you set up systems to lessen budget stress in the future. My only caution though, is not to pick someone who doesn't put a lot of time and effort into their own financial planning.

Allowing for a small emergency fund emergency (short-term savings) is a requirement if you want to succeed. Initially, you should favor putting together a small emergency fund even over paying down your large debt. Otherwise, you may be on track with getting rid of your debt, then an emergency will occur and deplete your gains and trash your budget. Life is full of emergencies, but it is only a real emergency if you have not prepared.

Now for a shocker: You can create a large income, but never create a high net worth, or even a positive net worth for that matter.

Income and wealth are not heavily correlated (related) due to the more important impact of financial behaviors such as budgeting.[10] Remember all the professional sports athletes who went broke right after their careers ended? I saw similar situations with my police officer peers who made great pay. Even when some of them were close to retirement, they could hardly pay their monthly bills. This is after having a steady job for 20 to 30 years. The opposite could be true as well. You can have a lower income compared to others and still create a high net worth. It is all a matter of what you do with your income.

If you are in a financial crisis, with serious debt problems, a traditional budget will not do. You have to ramp it up into emergency mode, but a crisis budget is temporary. You can't stay in crisis budget mode indefinitely. It will burn you out and you will stop budgeting. Set a specific date you will end the crisis budget. I always tell myself I can get through almost any hardship if it is temporary. To learn how to create a crisis budget, see the action steps in the workbook, located in the back of the book. Keep these aspects of a crisis budget in mind:

- Stay calm so you can come up with creative strategies, such as taking on a temporary roommate.
- Increase income (overtime, a second job, a business, etc.).
- Lower both your wants and needs.
- Possible consolidation of debts into lower payment plan

I have used a crisis budget several times and cleared significant debt after two separate divorces. If I can do it, then you certainly can as well. Go through the action steps for additional help with this issue.

Chapter 14 Summary Formulas

Income + Expenses + Time period = Budget

50% Fixed or Necessary Expenses + 30% Wants
Category + 20% Savings = 50/30/20 Budget

High Salary ≠ High Net Worth

Problem Debt = Crisis Budget

Chapter 15

From Money Disaster to Financial Prosperity

Answer the following questions.

My financial life is under control. (True/False)_____.
My personal life is under control. (True/False)_____.
My work life is under control. (True/False)_____.

> *Are you in control of your life? If your financial situation is your number-one stressor, that is a strong indication you are not.*

This book includes many true stories about people who have faced extreme adversity at some point in the past. Their troubling experiences impact their present by creating strong inner emotions that formed their subconscious emotions and beliefs. Their subconscious beliefs, in turn, fuel their actions. Multiple adverse childhood experiences (ACE) are highly related to later destructive lifestyle choices such as smoking, overeating, under-eating, excessive drinking, drug use and poor money management skills. ACE has also been shown to have a strong link to adult negative health conditions such as higher stress levels, lower fitness levels, various preventable health problems, lower social support and even a shorter life expectancy.

Money is not a separate aspect of our lives. Instead, money impacts everything in our lives. Our emotions surrounding money also impact our ability to think clearly and logically. We have learned that if your finances are a disaster, your thinking quickly becomes less efficient, your performance at work suffers, your relationships suffer and your physical and mental health suffers as well. We have also learned the inverse is equally true. If your mental or physical health is poor, your finances become much harder to manage.

That is why the Breakthrough Formula for Prosperity has proven to be so effective. The Breakthrough Formula is a sustainable, holistic methodology that involves changing your mindset to get control of both your life and your financial issues. It is a multidisciplinary approach that includes the theories of psychology, clinical counseling, personal finance, motivation, mental health, education and even philosophy.

Three Essential Elements of the Breakthrough Formula for Prosperity:

1. Eliminate self-defeating behaviors
   - Recognizing your subconscious thoughts that fuel your unhelpful behaviors
   - Reframing your negative thoughts about the past to a more positive, helpful experience
2. Goal Setting
3. Financial Education

No singular element in this formula has ever been routinely successful in creating significant financial behavioral changes without the other elements. Our success dramatically increases when we use all three elements together. This is why it is essential to deal with our life problems using a holistic approach. This is the path to lasting change and creating a happier and more satisfying life.

The Breakthrough Formula for Prosperity will allow you to gain control over your life through creating a goal-centered and purposeful existence. Control over your life, such as you can achieve it, is absolutely essential to your mental, physical and financial well-being. With control of your life in hand, you can set your own life purpose. A life of purpose provides more meaning and texture to our daily existence. It is the genesis of not only great accomplishments, but a happier and more fulfilling life. Remember, in Chapter 1, I said our goal is to fashion a life that makes us want to leap out of bed in the morning eager to get started with our days. The Breakthrough Formula for Prosperity is the methodology needed to create that life.

Chapter 15 Summary Formulas

Managing Life Problems +
Financial Education + Goal Setting =
Breakthrough Formula for Financial Prosperity

From Motivation to Action Steps
Workbook

Chapter 1 Workbook
From Money Disaster to Breakthrough Prosperity

Motivation Boost
From Jail to Wealth

B elow is a list of 10 people who went to jail or served prison time. These people changed their thinking, changed their habits and changed their attitudes. Although I am sure their journeys were difficult, they persevered. Likely, these people overcame or worked around many of the problems you are now facing. In addition, these men and women also overcame the burden and stigma of being ex-convicts.

Danny Trejo (now famous actor) started smoking marijuana when he was only eight years of age. By age 12, he was addicted to heroin and ran the streets of Los Angeles to acquire the drugs he craved. This behavior landed him in and out of juvenile detention facilities throughout his teens.

As a young adult, Trejo became an armed robber to support his drug habit. This ongoing behavior was extremely risky and provided Trejo a rush that went well with his heroin addiction. His violent behavior landed him in various California prisons. Trejo was once reported to have said he had been inside every prison within the Californian penal system.

Inside prison, Trejo continued his violent behavior. He began boxing and became the welterweight boxing champion of the California prison system. This made him quite a celebrity inside, and he used his celebrity status to start a protection racket to make money. Newer inmates had to pay him a stipend to remain healthy. He also continued using drugs while in prison.

His behavior finally reached a crisis point when he was thrown into solitary confinement for assaulting a guard with a rock during a prison riot. After a time in solitary, he realized he had to turn his life around and he needed to change. While in solitary, he began praying to God. He vowed to live a Christian life and set goals to turn his life around. When he was released from solitary confinement, he began a 12-step program that allowed him to get sober.

Daniel Manville: manslaughter; now an attorney who obtained two undergraduate degrees while locked up

Uchendi Nwani: drug dealer; now a barbershop owner and motivational speaker

Jeff Henderson: illegal drug dealer and manufacturer; now chef and supervises menu at Caesars Palace and best-selling author

50 Cent: drug dealer; got most of his education while in prison; now a rapper

Mark Brandon "Chopper": Armed robber; served time for robbery and assault; became a best-selling author by writing crime fiction/non-fiction

Frank William Abagnale Jr.: fraud forgery; now owns a security consulting firm

Eugene-Francois Vidocq: identity theft; investigator and inventor of the detective agency that formed the basis of the Sir Author Cannon Doyle's *Sherlock Holmes* novels and short stories

Frederick Hutson: drug trafficking; created a database to find inmates and help families communicate with their loved ones in prison

Mike Pisciotta: robbery and drug abuse; high-tech business coach

Action Step 1

Are You in Crisis?

The Depression Hotline is 888-640-5174 if you suffer from severe depression. Call that number if you can't wait to get in to see a mental health professional.

Call the suicide help line at 1-800-273-8255 if you have thoughts of harming yourself.

Action Step 2

More About ACE Study

1. ACE (Adverse Childhood Experiences) are traumatic events you may have suffered as a child. For example: were your parents alcoholics or physically or verbally abusive? These experiences impact you later in life and create self-defeating behaviors like

drinking to excess, smoking, drug use, lack of physical activity and an entire host of other self-sabotaging financial behaviors.

2. Take the ACE Quiz to see where you fall on the scale at https://www.npr.org/sections/health-shots/2015/03/02/387007941/ take-the-ace-quiz-and-learn-what-it-does-and-doesnt-mean

If you score 4 or higher on this quiz, you could suffer some pretty significant emotional problems later in life. A high score means toxic stress could have damaged the structure of a child's developing brain. This kind of stress creates psychological and even physical problems later in life.[15]

You can offset the above ACE test score with resilience factors that help you bounce back from childhood adverse incidents, stress, past traumatic events, life-threatening illnesses, adverse childhood experiences or just general life challenges. An example of a resilience factor is having someone who cares about you in your life or being involved in volunteer work in the community. See where you are now with the resilience score and learn more about increasing your resilience in the future. Take the test here: https://www. resiliency.com/free-articles-resources/the-resiliency-quiz/

Chapter 2 Workbook
From Past Money Disaster Stories to New Stories of Success

Motivation Boost
From Extreme Poverty or Bankruptcy to Wealth

George Crum: Crum was born in 1822 in New York State as George Wicks. His father was an African American and his mother was a native American from the Huron tribe. Wicks later changed his professional name to Crum which was his father's name when his father worked as a jockey. Crum made his early living as a hunting guide in Adirondack Mountains. He eventually became famous for his camp cooking on his guided hunting trips. This soon led to a well-paying job at Cary Moon's Lake House in Saratoga Springs where he worked with his sister, Catherine Wicks. The two were famous for their great cooking and drew visitors from all over the U.S.

Not everyone was an immediate fan. Legend has it that one day the Wicks siblings were trying to please a grumbling customer who kept complaining the French fries he was given were cut too thickly for his liking. Eventually, the Wicks became so frustrated that they cut shavings from their potatoes and fried them in oil—thereafter dubbed Saratoga Chips. The chips were an immediate hit at the restaurant.

Although Crum didn't patent the potato chip, nor did he attempt to distribute them nationwide, he did start his own restaurant called Crum's House, located in Malta, in Saratoga County. People from all over flocked to wait in line to get into his restaurant. Crum's House was famous for requiring the wealthy wait in line with the poor to enter his restaurant. He never played favorites! This made his food even more desirable by the wealthy clientele for its scarcity, and his restaurant was quite successful.

Walt Disney went from being bankrupt 1921 to a becoming a millionaire with the release of the film *Snow White* in 1937—a film he went into heavy debt to produce.

George Foreman: After squandering all the money he made, this two-time world boxing champion filed for bankruptcy. Yet, he came back by using his celebrity status to advertise the George Foreman Grill and is now estimated to be worth $200 million.

Larry Ellison went from being dirt poor and started a company with two other partners called Software Development Laboratories. Later, this company evolved into Oracle Systems.

Grant Cardone went from being broke to owning multiple businesses. He now teaches others how to create wealth.

Grace Groner a secretary at Abbott Labs who bought three shares of the company stock and invested a total of $180. The stock split many times, and she reinvested all dividends. At the time of her death, she was worth $7 million through her investing success.

P. T. Barnum was an orphan who grew up homeless and on the streets of Bethel, Connecticut. He became a businessman and entrepreneur. He went bankrupt several times throughout his life. Additionally, Barnum was a financial educator and writer. He used his earnings from financial education to dig himself out of bankruptcy each time. Barnum became a millionaire with his traveling circus in 1873.

Milton S. Hershey: This businessman and entrepreneur went out of business several times before setting up the Hershey Chocolate Company in 1900. He was worth $60 million at the time of his death.

Dani Johnson: In 1990, she was broke and living in her car. She started a weight loss company with a handwritten flyer and made $250,000 the first year. By the second year, she was a millionaire. She went on to become a multi-millionaire with numerous businesses.

Halle Berry: As a struggling actress, she went broke and was living in a homeless shelter. She later became a movie star in big hit movies. Even though her early experience was pretty horrible, Berry was able to reframe it into a training ground to help make herself mentally tough.

Ursula Burns grew up in a housing project in Manhattan. She went to college and became an intern at Xerox. Later, Burns became CEO and chairwoman of that company. She is currently a non-executive director of Diageo since April 2018 and a member of the board of directors at Uber. She is considered the most powerful business person in the world.

Action Step 1

Check the Money Scripts You Most Identify With:

- ☐ Having more money will solve all of my problems.
- ☐ More money will make me happy.
- ☐ To be safe, I need more money.
- ☐ I have to save every dime I can.
- ☐ I can save others with money.
- ☐ It is my job to save people with money.
- ☐ The rich are greedy.
- ☐ The rich are dishonest.
- ☐ The rich got their money by cheating others.
- ☐ I don't deserve to be happy.
- ☐ I am unworthy/failure.
- ☐ I am terrible with money.
- ☐ I can never be successful.
- ☐ The rich are unhappy.
- ☐ You should never talk about money.
- ☐ Money is not important in life.
- ☐ If I am good, more money will come my way.
- ☐ Women aren't good with money.
- ☐ Women aren't good leaders.
- ☐ Women need a husband to take care of them because finances are so complicated.
- ☐ Men are the breadwinners in the family
- ☐ Men are smart with money
- ☐ Men are leaders
- ☐ Others envy the things I have.
- ☐ My friends look up to me because I have cooler stuff than they do.
- ☐ Money burns a whole in my pocket.

Action Step 2

Reframing Your Defective Money Scripts

Don't let negative money scripts dictate your actions. This chapter illustrated how you can reframe your story and make it a positive lesson. We understand our lives from the perspective of the stories we tell ourselves. You can rewrite your past experiences into a positive lesson and tell yourself that story instead. Move your story from an experience you did not want to the important lessons you learned that helped you grow as a person. For example, instead of the money story "The rich are unhappy," you could reframe it to "Some wealthy people are happy and use their wealth to make our world a better place." Then find examples through research that proves your new story to be true and add those examples to the stories you tell yourself and others.

Examples of repaired money stories:

- It is okay for an average person to have money and a reasonable amount of wealth and comfort.
- I can control my money with a moderate amount of effort.
- If I want to get ahead, I can learn to do so and take the necessary action steps to achieve that goal.
- The system is ready and waiting for me to succeed.
- There are good and bad wealthy people. Some help others with their wealth and provide value to our society.
- My spending and savings must be in balance with both my financial goals and living my daily life.
- I don't need a partner to handle my money. I am a capable and strong person.
- If I don't want to be poor, I can direct my own life and achieve reasonable wealth and comfort.

- Spending money on something I need, want and can afford is okay and won't lead to poverty.
- If I spend some money on myself, and I can afford it, it does not mean I will be like my parent(s).
- Stuff you own doesn't matter. Your life balance, life purpose and actions are what matter.
- I can control myself and my actions. If I need help doing this, I will take action to obtain that help ASAP.

Action Step 3

Reduce Anxiety Surrounding Your Finances

You can get a money coach to help you with your finances, or you can ask a friend who is good with money to help coach you, or you can even solicit help from a credit counselor. What you are looking for is someone who will encourage you to be calm and relaxed and provide instruction and patience but also hold you accountable to do the things you discussed and agreed upon. Working with someone else on your budget frequently reduces budget stress and anxiety.

Did you know that when you get stressed that your IQ and problem-solving ability drops significantly? Money stress actually slows down your brain function.[9] Work first on reducing your stress and then work on your financial issues—or get help from a trusted friend or professional who is not stressed about their money situation to assist you.

Chapter 3 Workbook
From Financial Mishap to Goals of Abundance

Motivation Boost
Goal Setting Expert

B y this time, I can safely call myself an expert at setting and achieving the goals I've set. I have accomplished countless goals, including some pretty big personal ones like building significant wealth, my professional accomplishments and doing my part to create a strong marriage. One of the advantages I had in life was when I set specific goals. I was willing to work consistently (relentlessly my detractors would say) toward those goals. In the end, those accomplishments made me more knowledgeable, more flexible, more capable, and certainly more diverse. I also feel I can now take on just about anything and have a reasonably good chance of success. This is a long way mentally, physically and emotionally from where I began in my adult life so many years ago.

Action Step 1

For the Times Motivation is Lacking

We all have times when we are not motivated. I have labeled my periods where I lack motivation as "the suck." To me, the suck includes an accompanying blah feeling along with the lack of motivation. We all get it sometimes. I get past it by reducing my focus and completing just one task at a time. Usually, after I get started and concentrate on something else besides the suck pulling me down, my lack of motivation dissipates, and I can get on with my day. If it continues, I might give myself a short break from goal work and concentrate on diet and exercise to create more energy and a better mood.

The suck is most likely your brain's love of its habits and a reliance on routine. Your brain is trying to drag you back down to the safe status quo that was your life before. Even though your brain likes routine, you know intellectually you don't want to be in that place mentally or physically anymore. The old way no longer works for you, so set goals and move forward to make your life different and better. Success always lies just past the suck!

Action Step 2

Separate Goals from Daydreams

Goals have a specific structure. They are written and have benchmarks to measure your progress against. Get out your financial journal and do the following:

1. Write your well-considered, well-researched goal at the top of the page.
2. List the steps you must take to achieve this goal. Don't worry about how many steps or how much paper you use.
3. Put a date above each step that you want completed based on the step's difficulty and length of time it will take to accomplish.
4. Create a different page(s) for each goal.

5. As you work the process toward your goals, celebrate after each step is completed. Seriously! Even the simple steps require at least some celebration.
6. Post your goals where you can see them every day.
7. Move the goals you posted around your house or office so they don't fade into the background.

Chapter 4 Workbook
From Bad Habits to Prosperous Habits

Motivation Boost
Here is a New Formula for Your Consideration

Intrinsic Motivation + Internal Locus of Control +
Effort = Better Financial Habits

This sounds very complicated, and it could be made complicated. In fact, many books have been written on each component of the formula above. For our purposes, however, an internal locus of control simply means that you feel you have the power within yourself to change your habit(s). For example, if you want to save a few dollars every month for an emergency fund, you believe you have the power to control your financial outcomes and the ability to save a few dollars every month. If you want to stop spending, you believe it is totally within your power to change your habits and do so. You must feel you play a large role in creating all the outcomes you experience in life. In short, you have a feeling of "I can do it!"

Intrinsic motivation implies you internally value both the habit change and the behaviors you will need to develop to build personal wealth. For example, you believe it is important (in and of itself) for you to become debt free, and there is psychological and spiritual value in being frugal on your way to this goal. You also value the outcome (more wealth) because it will provide you and your loved ones with more options and resources in the near future.

If you value the outcome because it will make your spouse happy, however, you have much less of a chance of successfully changing your habit(s). The further your motivation moves away from your personal desire to achieve the outcome, the less likely it is that you will be successful.[10] In short you must believe accomplishing the goal is important!

Another success factor linked to your motivation to create habit changes includes the amount of effort you are willing to expend to accomplish your habit-change goal. What are you willing to do? The more effort and energy you are willing to expend to change your bad habit(s), the better chance of success you have.[11] In fact, it is a well-known motivational axiom that those who succeed are willing to do things that others are not willing to do.

The amount of effort you are willing to expend is also directly proportional to your intrinsic motivation and your locus of control. In effect, these three motivational concepts create a feedback loop where each factor depends upon the others. When these three factors are in alignment, very little can stop you for long. You become a juggernaut to success.

Action Step 1

Obtain Assistance

Call and make an appointment with a psychologist or therapist today. It may take a while to get in. Going to your appointment is worthwhile because psychologists are experts at helping people change dysfunctional financial behaviors. There are treatment methods available to help you change your habits and deal with other issues that might be holding you back. Various treatment regimens have been repeatedly shown to help you reduce stress, anxiety and depression and improve your financial health.[12]

Action Step 2

Habits That Will Improve Your Life and Finances

    A. Exercise is one of the most productive habits you can have. Once you begin exercising, you have more energy, you feel better about yourself, you reduce stress, you reduce anxiety and your performance in many other areas of your life starts to improve. You will be more energized, which means you will spend less and pay more attention to your finances. Your plate will not feel quite as full, so you have more emotional capacity to work on financial issues without stressing out.

    B. An important fundamental habit is to set financial goals that you and your partner agree upon. Create your own action steps to reach your goal(s). Your goals should definitely include your combined vision of money.

    C. Read, learn and explore new ideas. In finances, knowledge is power! You can never know enough. Keep reading and keep learning and thinking about what you've learned and how you could apply those lessons to your life and financial performance.

    D. Understand that investing your wages (a fundamental habit) is only one way to create wealth. There are many other ways to do it. The more diverse your knowledge in finances, the more secure you become.

Examine all your future spending and purchases with the mindset of: Will this purchase add value to my life?

Chapter 5 Workbook
From Overspending to Financial Freedom

Motivation Boost
People Who Conquered Excess Spending

Cait Flanders graduated from college with what she characterizes as a shopping addiction and $23,000 in credit card debt. She had a sudden realization that none of the purchases she was making were bringing her fulfillment or happiness. As a moderately paid government employee, Cait knew her life needed to change. This led to a year of buying only necessities, simplifying her life and the banishment of all shopping. Soon, Cait realized the less she bought the more fulfilled and free she felt. After clearing up her debt and stopping her spending, Cait unfortunately relapsed into her shopping behavior again when she became stressed due to life events, like a breakup with her boyfriend and her parents' divorce. She fought through again and now understands herself even more.

Antoinette Russell: Writer and mother overcame her spending problem and now has a strong marriage and is more prosperous

Mary Hunt: Writer and entrepreneur who paid off her debts for 13 years and now has debt freedom

Olivia Mellan: Former overspender, now a money coach and a psychotherapist who currently has her spending under control

Buzz Bissinger: A prize-winning journalist, bestselling author admitted to being an overspender who struggles with his shopping/spending problem daily

Action Step 1

Emergency Procedures for Crippling Debt

Being successful at completing even a single action step can begin to change everything! Success at change begins to alter your internal script by building confidence, self-esteem and increasing your self-efficacy. You start to feel like you can control your destiny. One small change has the power to make a huge difference in your life.

A. Suspend your credit cards until you pay off the bills.

B. Contact one of the below organizations for immediate assistance. The organizations below have been found to be effective for over-spending behaviors:

- Debtors Anonymous
- Spenders Anonymous (online shopping addiction support group)

C. Ask your bank for help or a referral for credit counseling. One-on-one credit counseling has been shown to improve persistent spending behaviors.

D. Get a prepaid credit card, and only use only that card.

E. Set up rewards within your budget where you can make purchases, within budgetary limits, but only if you follow the budget you created.

F. Create more social interaction(s) to take your mind off of spending and the stress of your finances.

G. Those who focus more on the future are able to have more success with their finances.

H. Work on being grateful for the good things you have in your life right now. This reduces stress and increases your positive thinking.

I. Is there a way you can begin to simplify your life?

J. Paying an overspender's or debtor's bills is a losing proposition for changing future behaviors. This approach adds to the problems by making the person you are trying to help even more helpless. You become an enabler or a participant in the dysfunctional emotions. In fact, family members bailed Joann (discussed at the beginning of Chapter 5) out a couple of times, and her behavior still continues. If you are trying to overcome this problem, do not ask others to bail you out. Solving this problem is part of the process of healing.

Chapter 6 Workbook
From Underspending to Financial Security

Motivation Boost
From Miser to Balance

"The Miser Robs Himself." — *Johann Kaspar Lavater*

One of the world's most recognized underspending misers is Ebenezer Scrooge. Mr. Scrooge is a fictional, literary character created by Charles Dickens in his book *A Christmas Carol.*[2] In Dickens' story, Scrooge is fortunate in that by examining his past he is finally able to feel the emotions he had deeply suppressed during his childhood many years ago. Once he understands his past and the feeling that flowed from his unhappy experiences, he is able to release his trapped emotions from his past and change his current behaviors.

In the story, the miserly Scrooge is first visited on Christmas Eve by three Christmas ghosts who help him review his life. The first ghost, The Ghost of Christmas Past, takes Scrooge on a trip back to his early life. Scrooge sees his childhood and soon feels the heart-wrenching sadness of being abandoned by his father at a boarding school. He was left without love, attention or his father's approval. At the same time these events were happening his sister was cared for at home and greatly loved by his father. For Scrooge, this was a severe adverse childhood experience that damaged him emotionally. These feelings were so painful, Scrooge evidently repressed them and most of his other emotions. Finally, after feeling those painful emotions stemming from his childhood memories (and other painful incidents in his life revealed by the other Christmas ghosts), he is freed in both his heart and his mind from his terrible emotional burdens. His new understanding allows Scrooge to give up his underspending behavior, miserly attitude toward life and his total disregard for the welfare of others. Scrooge also reflects upon his own well-being, his future, what he wants from his life and how he wishes to be remembered. He decides he did not want to live and die being despised by everyone he knows. With these realizations, he becomes a reformed underspender and a happier man who takes new joy in his life and in his satisfying relationships with others.[3]

Scrooge was lucky. Most underspenders never have such an earth-shattering epiphany. They see nothing wrong with their extreme underspending behaviors. They rarely seek to change their world view, even when it is clearly demonstrated to them their underspending is wrong and is harming both themselves and those they love. Change comes slow to underspenders, but is worth striving for. The miserly underspenders are missing out on what life could offer them.

Action Step 1

A Practical Test

To determine if you have a problem with underspending and should consider changing your thinking and resulting behaviors, do the following two things this month:

1. Take a friend or family member to lunch and pay for the lunch.

2. Buy a small treat or extravagance for yourself—something you want, but would not normally spend money on. For example, you might purchase a latte at a coffee shop or maybe go to a movie theater to watch a movie.

If you have anxiety surrounding these two assigned tasks and are unable to complete them, you likely have a problem with underspending. No improvement can occur unless you first admit that you likely need to alter your world view and some of your accompanying behaviors that support your money-equals-safety view of your world.

Action Step 2

Discussion or Journal Questions

Journal or discuss the following questions with someone to better understand your underspending behaviors:

1. Do you understand what situations in your past might cause you to have anxiety with spending money?

2. Are relationships with family and friends important to you? Research consistently shows that to have a happy or fulfilling life, the answer to this question is always yes! What can you do to begin reinforcing or rebuilding your relationships today?

3. What makes you happy besides saving money? To have a happy and/or fulfilling life there needs to be an activity/hobby you enjoy doing.

4. What would you do if you had only six months to live?

5. Are you willing to change your underspending behaviors? Why or why not?

Chapter 7 Workbook
From Financial Infidelity to Relationship Harmony

Motivation Boost
Couples Who Got Rich Together

My wife and I are a millionaire couple who created our wealth from scratch. To convey the full range of our accomplishment, I'll mention we were both divorced twice previously when we got together. Because of our previous experiences, we knew that shared goals were the key to financial success from the very start of our marriage.

My 32-year police career began at the Dayton, Ohio Police Department in 1981. I began saving money and investing with my first paycheck at a rate of $50 every paycheck—paid every two weeks. I was promoted through the ranks and eventually retired as a major in my police department.

I met my wife, Lisa, at a local hospital emergency room where she worked as a certified emergency nurse. We were married a year later. Lisa had also been saving since her first paycheck as a nurse. We immediately set a goal of achieving financial independence early in our lives together. At first, our efforts resulted in marginal success. After reviewing our progress, we began researching and learning more about budgeting, saving and investing. We frequently spent evenings taking turns reading financial books to each other or reading books independently and providing a summary of the books to one another. The newly gained knowledge proved to be just the encouragement we needed. We soon achieved outstanding success and created financial abundance.

At the same time, we raised three boys to become financially successful adults. We retired from our jobs in our mid-fifties and are financially independent. Now, we set our own schedules, come and go as we wish and travel extensively across the U.S. and abroad.

I became a Certified Financial Education Instructor, financial coach, author and speaker. I also wrote and published books, including *Messages From Your Future: The Seven Rules For Financial, Personal, and Professional Success* [7] and *The Illustrated Guide to Financial Independence.*[8] I am actively involved in the community and have a newer life goal to spread financial literacy to improve my community, state and nation. I've taught and presented financial independence classes to the Dayton Police Academy, at Sinclair Community College, at Miami Valley Hospital and at the Travis County Jail where I teach financial skills to prisoners. I have never sold financial investments of any kind. My mission is strictly to increase financial literacy for individuals, and most of my classes are free to interested parties.

The Moore family reached financial independence through frugal spending, planning and working together to reach their goals. Although becoming a millionaire couple was not their specific goal, creating financial independence was. The couple became millionaires in 2018. They achieved their goal in their early fifties.

Helen and Jeff Brown are multi-millionaires who live in Indianapolis, Indiana. They created their wealth by concentrating on the basics of creating income, saving and then investing. They used mutual funds as their primary investment vehicles. They like a mix of investments that equal about 60% of their investments in stocks mutual funds and 40% in bond funds.

Do Won Chang and his wife Jin Sook are on the *Forbes* list of wealthiest Americans. After immigrating from Korea, the couple immediately began working at whatever jobs they could get. Chang worked at three low-paying jobs, and while working for these low wages, the couple decided to open a clothing store. They saved their money, and with an $11,000 investment, they opened their first clothing store. With hard work and by always looking for opportunities in this field, the couple soon built a chain of clothing stores (Forever 21). Their shrewd businesses skills enabled them to obtain a net worth of an estimated three billion dollars, a long way from scrapping together the $11,000 to start their first clothing store.

Jeff and Dee who live in Atlanta, Georgia have a net worth of over two million dollars. It was a journey to get there, and they made their share of mistakes along the way. For example, Jeff became an overspender for a while and put the two of them into debt. Later, Dee took a turn and became a secret spender and hid her expenses from Jeff. As time passed, however, the couple overcame their dysfunctional money stories and resulting habits. Once they did that, they moved rapidly toward success and wealth.

Action Step 1

Steps for Couples Regarding Money

1. Set goals with your significant other. This is one of the most important steps. If you are not on the same page today, that doesn't mean you cannot get on the same page in the future. The heart of this entire matter revolves around creating jointly agreed-upon, long-term, mid-term and short-term goals that excite you. Maybe you can have a romantic dinner date to discuss goals. That will at least get the conversation started. Eventually, the goals have to be written down and the path mapped forward.

2. Write it down. Both of you should write about your goals and dreams in your financial journals and compare notes.

3. Talk it out. Consider couples counseling/therapy if a problem persists. Therapists deal with couple/money issues all the time.

4. If it is a matter of not knowing what to do, consider hiring a money coach to assist you in getting your journey started. If you don't want to hire a coach, consider getting help from a credit counselor or a financial planner at your credit union or bank.

5. Knowledge is power in the financial world. As you can see from my story above, my wife and I spent considerable time together reading, learning and using the knowledge we gained.

6. Focus on your partner's strengths, not his or her weaknesses. Great teams concentrate on using their teammates' strengths and delegate areas of weakness.

7. Celebrate financial victories, even small ones!

8. If I have learned anything from my past, it is that you must be your own independent person. To have a better spouse, you must strive to be a better person yourself.

9. Marriage is a team sport! Be a team player.

Action Step 2

End Financial Infidelity

1. Get couples counseling ASAP. Follow the directions of a properly trained and certified therapist/counselor.

2. The offending partner should consider what he or she wants out of life and the relationship. Where are you headed? Write in your financial journal about why you might be exhibiting financial infidelity behaviors.

3. Answer the following questions in your journal: Do I want to save this relationship? What am I willing to do to save it?

4. Get a debt counselor to assist you.

Action Step 3

End Financial Enabling by a Family Member

1. Stop enabling the family member! Perhaps contribute less each month until you reach zero dollars or give them a date when the enabling will stop outright.

2. You and your partner should present a unified front to the family member. The goal is to move this person from dependence to independence. Even though he or she may view this as an attack, it is actually the best help you can give. Stay strong.

3. Improve the skills of the financially enabled family member. If he or she will not take direction from you

or your partner, enlist the help of a financial coach or debt counselor.

4. You and your partner should present a unified front to avoid responding to guilt trips, emotional blackmail, insults or even outright threats. Be prepared for significant pushback.

5. Never waver or change your mind about ending your financial support for a family member, or the money demands will never stop.

6. Seek counseling if this causes significant problems with you personally or between you and your partner.

Chapter 8 Workbook
From Under-Earning to Joyous Work

Motivation Boost
People Who Left Under-Earning Behind

Emily Williams is an author and success coach. Her life changed after she finished her undergraduate degree in psychology. She was on her way to Chicago to attend a graduate school there when she had a minor meltdown about the path she had chosen in life. She changed her mind and decided this path was not the right way for her to go. She moved back in with her parents for a while until she could determine what she really wanted in life.

She moved from her small hometown in Ohio to the UK. She was determined to follow her dreams. She lived in a hostel and got several jobs to start out her new life. She began a coaching and success business when she was $120k in debt with school loans and significant, high-interest credit card debt. Within a year, she had a thriving business making six figures. She has made a great life for herself in the UK, is now married and is living the life of her dreams. Emily says, "Why not you? If others can do it, then so can you!"

Barbara Stanny is the heiress of H&R Block mogul Richard Block. She ended up marrying a man who engaged in financial infidelity via secret gambling. He lost big money—all of it hers, of course. By the time she figured out what was going on and managed to get a divorce, she owed over one million dollars in back taxes and her ex-husband had decimated many of her financial resources.

She now warns people about the risk of allowing your spouse to control your finances without your participation and involvement. Her story shows that ignorance about your money is very dangerous. She has championed overcoming financial illiteracy that holds so many people back. Later a friend and mentor told her she was an habitual under-earner. Of course, Barbara denied it, and after thinking about it for a while, she realized her friend was right. She was overly dependent upon her inheritance.

Barbara has changed her life and has conquered her underearning behaviors and habits. She just wrote the book *Overcoming Underearning: A Five-Step Plan to a Richer Life.*[12] Stanny is now a financial therapist and wealth coach and has left underearning behind.

Action Step 1

Are You An Under-Earner?
Take this test to determine if you are an under-earner: https:// harpers.org/2012/05/the-underearners-test/

Action Step 2

Quote For Thought
Think about how this quote might apply to you.

"Thoughts become perception, perception becomes reality. Alter your thoughts, alter your reality."

—William James

Action Step 3

How to Better Reframe Your Story

In previous chapters, we talked about altering your money story by incorporating the positive lessons you learned from unpleasant memorable events in your life. Your thoughts form your identity about who you believe you are. In most cases, your view of your past events changes naturally with both imperfect recall, and your present-day experiences provide you with new perspectives. With new experiences, you gain new insights, which change your view of your past. Those with adverse childhood experiences, however, are more resistant to these natural changes because of all the emotions that are integrated into the memories.

Dr. Benjamin Hardy says that reframing your story to a positive message helps your brain tell yourself a different story that serves your life much better. Also, use this new positive story and experience to measure past events against the progress in life you have made since the event(s).[13]

Action Step 4

Practice Positive Self-talk

According to the Mayo Clinic, one of the best ways to turn negative thinking into positive thinking is to practice positive self-talk. They suggest starting by following one simple rule: Don't say anything to yourself that you wouldn't say to anyone else.[14]

Action Step 5

Try These Steps to Change Your Story

    A. You can change just a few words in the story you tell yourself to make it more positive.

    B. Figure out what you want in life.

    C. Say this mantra often, "I deserve good things! Why *not* me?"[15]

Chapter 9 Workbook
From Money Avoidance to Embracing Financial Planning

Motivation Boost
People Who Overcame Money Avoidance

Gandhi said, "Capital is not evil; it is its wrong use that is evil. Capital in some form or another will always be needed."

Edmund Burke said, "If we command our wealth, we shall be rich and free. If our wealth commands us, we are poor indeed."

Erica Wong graduated with a degree in civil engineering and $90k in school debt. She started her new entry-level job in the New York City area and had to overcome a huge cost of living in this region. She felt she would live her entire life in debt and wanted to find a different path. Rather than just going with the flow like everyone else, she devised a financial plan to get herself out of debt as quickly as possible. Her plan had her living on a mere $13 a day after she paid her bills and paid down her debt. Wong said it was brutal for the first year and was almost depressing. She knew this was her path, however, if she ever wanted a life where she was not a slave to her debt. As often happens, her journey became easier as she progressed. She paid off her school debt in less than five years.

Nicole Rule used to be a big-time budget avoider. She did everything she could to avoid working on either her or her husband's finances. The couple made little effort to control their spending. Nicole's primary hobby was going on shopping excursions to Target. After she and her husband had their second child, however, she realized things had to change fast. The couple had accumulated $100k in consumer debt. She understood that they were going to be broke forever unless they developed a plan to improve their spending and finances. She developed a financial plan based on the couple's long-term goals and values. The couple funded what was important to them while cutting spending. She and her husband paid off their outstanding debt and now she is a stay-at-home mom. She began her own financial coaching business to help other people successfully do the same thing she accomplished.

Neil Ellington works for a nonprofit credit counseling agency. He helps people who have various money and credit problems. Neil says that one of his clients has what he calls a "Messiah complex" and rejects the income he receives from his job because others have minimal financial resources. The client, in service of the poor, has accumulated credit card debt in the area of $14k and is now having trouble paying off the bill. The client used this money mostly for meals to feed the homeless and assisting his church to serve the needs of the local homeless population. Neil is helping the client design an overall financial plan to pay down his debt and trying to help him understand that with a financial plan and sound financial footing, rather than always being broke, he will be able to help even more people.

The Cordovas had a dream to run a bed and breakfast. After years of saving and financial planning, the couple made their dreams come true. They now own Alpen Way Chalet Mountain, a wonderful bed and breakfast in Colorado.

Action Step 1

Financial Planning & Goals

Those who complete a written financial plan and take action on that plan are more likely to accomplish their goals and create better financial outcomes.

1. Set a date to start your financial plan now.
2. Set a date to complete your plan.
3. Work on the plan every day until completed.

Action Step 2

Overcome Budget Avoidance

For those with budget avoidance behaviors, creating a detailed financial plan can create stress. Finding someone to assist you can lighten the mood. Consider doing the following:

A. Hire a financial coach to help you.
B. Work on the financial plan with your partner.
C. A financial planner will usually help you for an hourly fee, or sometimes the plan will be free if you use them for investing. FYI: most usually don't go down to the budget level of planning.
D. Recruit a financial buddy to help you construct a financial plan. Pick someone who isn't judgmental and is smart enough not to talk about your finances to others.

    E. A nonprofit credit counseling group will help you construct a financial plan. Look for one in your area.

    F. Debtors Anonymous will also help you change your financial habits.

Action Step 3

Imagine Your Future

Psychology Today reported on a Stanford University study that showed looking at an aged photo of yourself increases your willingness to save money. Go to one of the apps that allow you to age your photo and look into your future. Looking at aged photos has been shown to increase savings and budgeting behaviors.[18]

Action Step 4

Discover Your Money Personality

Take a quiz to find out what money personality you have here: https://bit.ly/3uaPyZE

Action Step 5

Look At Other Financial Plans

Sample financial plans, financial planning templates and other examples are here: https://bit.ly/3ukxDjl

Chapter 10 Workbook
From Helplessness to Optimistic Action

Motivation Boost
People Who Became Optimists

G lenn Stearns may be the ultimate optimist! He came from a very poor family with alcoholic parents; he was dyslexic and he did very poorly in school. Most of Glenn's peers ended up drug addicted or in prison. Glenn wanted more out of his life. A mentor helped Glenn get started and inspired him. Soon, Glenn was off and running with his various businesses. Eventually, through hard work, he became a billionaire.[18]

One of the most inspiring TV shows I have ever seen was a show called *Undercover Billionaire*, produced by the Discovery Channel. In this reality TV show, Glenn Stearns (55 years old) believed and boasted that he could put together a company worth a million dollars in only 90 days starting from nothing. His philosophy is that with his knowledge, he could start over if he had to.[19] Now that is certainly self-confidence, self-efficacy, and a crazy amount of optimism.

So, Glenn stared with only one hundred dollars in cash and an old truck given to him by Discovery Channel. The show sent him to Erie, Pennsylvania, where he knew no one, and no one knew him. He had no place to stay initially and lived in the old truck. He completed the challenge, but he just barely managed it within the ninety-day period. Glenn said it was a lot easier at 25 than it was for him at 55. He faced so much hardship; most people would have given up. He even got pneumonia from living in his truck during the Erie, Pennsylvania winter.

I recommend checking out the show *Undercover Billionaire*, as it was truly inspiring and worth the watch.

Action Step 1

Change Your Long-term Mindset to Become More Positive.

A. Decide to be more optimistic.[20] It all starts with setting goals. If one of your goals is to be optimistic, you can make progress by consciously changing your thought patterns. This takes practice and will not happen overnight.

B. Consider taking up a martial art. This practice is famous for boosting a person's self-confidence. Self-confidence (belief that you can handle problems as they arise) is associated with higher self-efficacy (belief that you can control your life outcomes). Higher self-efficacy and higher self-confidence are associated with increased optimism and a much happier life. A martial art also provides you with physical fitness, activity and practical skills for everyday life.

C. When things go badly, recall instances where plans have gone well in the past. Remind yourself that this setback is temporary. In most cases, you control how much effort you expend toward success. Remember, you are powerful and have accomplished many things in the past.

D. Concentrate on your goals. Goals and goal achievement are the foundation of a more positive, optimistic, resilient, and happy life. Goal achievement gives you a higher internal locus of control, which improves your optimism, your self-esteem, and your ability to succeed.

E. Help other people! Particularly, help other people accomplish their own goals. Nothing makes you feel better, more positive, more confident or more competent than helping others achieve their dreams.

F. Pay attention to who you hang around with. Are your friends and family pessimistic or optimistic? Are your friends accomplished or just going with the flow? Seek to spend time with friends and family who are optimistic and successful and who are supportive of your goals. Be sure to support them in return.

G. Remember, pessimism and depression are linked. If you are depressed, it is difficult to be optimistic. See your health provider or a psychologist for an action plan if you are depressed. Work through some of the steps listed here to try to become more positive.

H. Think in terms of creating solutions and not about your problems. You get more of what you think about the most because it directs your thoughts, attitudes and actions. Those who come up with solutions far outperform people who only see the problems in front of them.

Action Step 2

Stop Your Negative Mindset

Seligman identified two effective ways to change a negative mindset when you identify your reaction as being negative. He calls the two techniques disputation and distraction.[21]

1. Disputation: This is when you question the reality of your negative thoughts about an event (or even about an anxious thought that keeps circling in your brain). In other words, you argue with yourself and mentally put forth your arguments. "Are my thoughts about this event actually based on facts and reality?" If not, you put forth the possible evidence for your improved way of thinking. "Is this an emotional reaction I am having to this event?" Mentally put forth your evidence that your feelings about this event may not be based on facts and actual reality. What could be another explanation instead of negative, overgeneralized thoughts? Seligman says that arguing with yourself can be surprisingly effective.

2. Distraction: Seligman discovered you can interrupt your negative thought patterns by distraction. The specific technique involves slamming your palm against a wall and yelling, "Stop!" This will temporarily stop the circling negative thought patterns. Then go on to another task to distract yourself further.

Action Step 3

Create a Positive Mindset

Take two minutes every day to write down things you are grateful for in your financial journal. This habit was shown to increase optimism significantly, and the impact would usually last throughout the day.[22]

Chapter 11 Workbook
From Going With the Flow to Pursuing a Life's Purpose

Motivation Boost
People Who Achieved Their Life Purpose

Part 1

Iddo Landau is a philosophy professor at Haifa University in Israel and writes about life purpose. According to Landau, people get hung up on what is missing from their lives rather than what they have. For example, most of the people he asked if their life had purpose said either "no" or believed their lives had little meaning. Landau believed these people did not create the success they wanted (in whatever field or area they were working in), so they gave up. However, you can always change your purpose in life, and it can be something as simple as your domestic relationships, volunteering to help others or even artistic pursuits. Many activities or hobbies in life can provide you with your life purpose. Most people miss the boat because they are stuck on one definition or idea about their life purpose.[11] As always, you are only limited by your thinking!

Taikichiro Mori became rich when he changed his life purpose at the age of 51. He quit his job as an economics professor and became a successful real estate investor and builder.

Franny Martin changed her life purpose and then became rich at the age of 70. She left her corporate job and started a preservative-free cookie baking and delivery service. Truly, her life passion has been hugely successful.

Part 2

Life Purpose Quotes:

"The sole meaning of life is to serve." — Leo Tolstoy

"Strive not to be a success, but rather to be of value." — Albert Einstein

"The purpose of our lives is to be happy." — Dalai Lama

"The purpose of life is a life of purpose." — Robert Byrne

"Work gives you meaning and purpose, and life is empty without it." — Stephen Hawking

"Love was life's secret purpose." — Martine Murray

"I believe purpose is something for which one is responsible; it's not divinely assigned." — Michael J. Fox

"There is no greater gift you can receive than to honor your calling. It's why you were born. And how you become most truly alive." — Oprah Winfrey

"Great minds have purposes, others have wishes."
— Washington Irving

"If you can't figure out your purpose, figure out your passion. For your passion will lead you right into your purpose."
— Bishop T. D. Jakes

Action Step 1

Find Your Life Purpose

Grab your financial journal and list the following:

A. What do you enjoy talking about the most?
B. What are the things that interest you the most?
C. What can you do to serve/help the cause you are most passionate about while serving yourself simultaneously?

Action Step 2

Tool to Help You Find Your Life Purpose

Take the "What's Your True Passion" test by UK magazine *Psychologies* to help you determine what your value is and how that impacts your life purpose. https://www.psychologies.co.uk/test-whats-your-true-passion

Chapter 12 Workbook
From Indecision to Financial Confidence

Motivation Boost
People Who Increased Their Self Confidence

You can succeed no matter your background if you have the correct mindset. Take Mary Ellen Pleasant, for example. Stories on her life vary because she worked with the underground railroad and abolitionists. She was born into slavery, moved to Massachusetts and was hired as part of the household staff of a well-to-do white family. She spent her time and energy saving and investing her wages during her time there.

It is reported that Ms. Pleasant then moved to San Francisco at the age of 39 during the gold rush. She managed to get a job as the household manager of a wealthy family. As the household manager, she did her best to fade into the background so she could overhear conversations and gather intelligence. Of much interest to her were conversations between the man of the house and his friends and family regarding investments or new gold mine discoveries. She used this insider information to purchase goldmine shares, stocks, real estate and small businesses. She amassed a fortune.

Mary Ellen Pleasant became the first self-made African-American millionaire and had a net worth of around thirty-million dollars. She used the money to help finance the local underground railroad and supported abolitionists all across the country. She continued working after she was wealthy to gain this intelligence information for both investing and to help blacks flee southern states to greater freedom.[8]

Action Step 1

Putting the Steps Together

    A. In your financial journal, list the five steps needed to create financial independence and how to apply them to your life.

    B. List the roadblocks you expect to encounter and how to overcome them.

Action Step 2

Spend Money Now Mindset

Do you have a spend-money-now mindset? If you won three million dollars, what is the first thing you'd do with that money? Do you think about all the amazing things you could buy? Do you want to buy a new home, a car or gift some money to help your family and friends? If those are your first thoughts, you likely have a spend-money-now mindset. It is not your fault, this is how our society has trained us all to think. You must now train yourself to think differently.

    When I think of having three million dollars, I immediately think about all the additional money I could make. With that kind of cash, I can easily produce over $200k a year in income by making very conservative investments. Then, I could spend the $200k however I like. The great thing is that $200k will come to me forever. It will come to me for my lifetime and well beyond it—assuming my relatives don't kill the golden goose. Also, by only taking such a small amount, I can still grow that three-million-dollar investment portfolio into an even larger sum. I want to grow it so annually it will make even more money for my use. That way, my annual income keeps rising.

Action Step 3

Opportunity Costs

A. The average credit card interest rate is 20.14%.

B. Using that rate, if you owe $5,000, your monthly payment = $200 for 11 years.

C. Minimum payment total = $8,500 over 11 years

D. You lose not only the $8,500, but you also lost the opportunity for the $8,500 to be paid to your investment accounts where each payment multiples exponentially over time.

Chapter 13 Workbook
From Culturally Restricted Thinking to a Growth Mindset

Motivation Boost
People Who Think Outside the Box

Part 1

I have a police friend we will call Jack who is comfortably wealthy. Jack really isn't that much of an investor, but he was an income stream developer extraordinaire. Jack, like me, started his career as a police officer. Jack soon developed an interest in investigating accidents, which was something most police officers disliked. He soon secured a job with our department's Traffic Investigative Unit and began investigating serious accidents, usually involving fatalities. Jack's reputation grew in the state as an excellent accident investigator and an accident reconstruction specialist.

Jack capitalized on this skill and soon began teaching accident investigation and accident reconstruction to college students at our local community college. He taught hundreds of students basic and advanced accident investigation and reconstruction. He also did some expert testimony training. He taught these and other subjects for years at the community college.

Jack eventually retired from the police department, but he continued working in this field by starting his own business that specialized in accident investigations and accident reconstruction work. He now employs other accident reconstructions specialists in his company. His business is in high demand and is sought out by many law firms and insurance companies. Jack retired in his early sixties. He now only works on projects or with businesses he wants to be involved in. He doesn't worry about money because he has multiple income streams flowing from these sources:

- Police Pension
- State of Ohio Teacher's Pension
- His accident reconstruction business
- Expert testimony training business
- His wife's job(s) and income

Jack never learned a lot about investing. Instead, he perfected the strategy of creating income streams to fund his life.

Part 2

People With A Disability Who Became Rich

Below is a list of people with disabilities who used their unique talents and abilities and created their own income streams. Some of them became quite wealthy.

Ralph Braun/muscular dystrophy: Designed and produced the first wheelchair-accessible van and founder of Braun Corporation.

Paul Orfalea, ADHD and dyslexia: owns FedEx and Kinko's

Kirk Keating/wheelchair-bound: owns a motor coach equipped with gaming equipment for party rental

Diane Grover/deaf: started a brand of coffee, jams and other food items sold in independent stores

Richard Branson/dyslexia: Virgin records and Virgin Empire brand

Action Step 1

Side Gigs to Create More Income

1. Ask for a raise.
2. Do freelance work as your primary gig or maybe as a side gig.
3. Provide coaching in areas in which you are an expert.
4. Buy and resell consumer items for a profit.
5. Start a business with little or no money on the side such as:
   a. Provide "bathroom detailing." Clean bathrooms inside businesses (employees typically do not want to do it).
   b. Become a rideshare driver.
   c. Become a dog walker.
   d. Spray paint house numbers on curbs.
   e. Make YouTube videos on subjects you like.
   f. Pressure wash trashcans to clean them.
   g. Pressure wash driveways and patios.
   h. Paint residential fences.

Action Step 2

Business Plan

If you want to start your own business, it is essential you have a business plan and a clear idea of how your business will work to create a profit. You can get this from your local SCORE office or score.org. SCORE can help you build a business plan from scratch, provide you with a mentor, in some cases help you find funding and provide you with some much-needed business training. This service is entirely free for veterans and a reasonable fee for everyone else. Contact your local SCORE office to get you up and running correctly. Even if your business is already up and running, SCORE can help you improve it.

Action Step 3

Discover Your Strengths

Get the most out of life and finances and use your skills, strengths and abilities to succeed. Learn what your greatest strengths are from the University of Pennsylvania Authentic Happiness Strength Inventory Test. https://www.authentichappiness.sas.upenn.edu/user/login?destination=node/423

Action Step 4

Be Like Robert Kiyosaki

Robert Kiyosaki (self-made millionaire, author, lecturer and inventor) is famous for bringing a very narrow definition of an asset to the American middle class. An asset is only something "that puts money into your pocket."[13] Buying high-priced items (cars, boats, homes, and condos) does not create income. Instead, these are consumer items that you pay for, usually on credit. There is little to no return on your investment or ROI.

Did you know that many of the so-called assets you own can actually have a negative value? If you bought a new car and put only a little money down on that car and created a loan for the remainder, you would likely owe more on the vehicle than it is worth. When you steer that car off the new car lot you bought it from, it can lose up to 33% of its book value as you drive home. Should you have an accident on the way home, and the vehicle is destroyed, did you know you would likely owe more on the vehicle than insurance could pay you for it because it is now a used vehicle and is now worth significantly less than you paid for it?

Surprisingly, even a home can become a negative asset. If you buy a house at a normal market price, for example, and suddenly we have a severe real estate price crash (real estate or home values can crash like the stock market), you would owe more on your house than it is worth. Such downturns usually involve the entire economy and likely would soon negatively impact your job. Should you be laid off or lose your job, you would likely be unable to make the payments on your home. Now you have to sell it and it could now easily be worth less than you owe. This is what kicked off the Great Recession in 2008.

Home values also have an inverse relationship to the number of available buyers. The more expensive the home you purchase, for example, the fewer the number of people who can afford to buy your home from you later. The less expensive your home, the more buyers in the population that can afford to buy your home when you decide to sell it. This is a fact that is really obvious during an economic downturn.

Other consumer items that are famous for creating a debt that exceeds their value include boats, motorcycles, collector items and the infamous timeshare purchase. People pay through the nose for these items, and they lose one-third to half of their value right after they purchase them. In some cases, like a timeshare for example, most people end up paying just to get out of them!

The point is, consumer items (even your home) are not really assets at all, despite their official definition as such. An asset, honestly and truly, is only something that creates a ROI for you.[14] For example, if you purchased a second home to rent and then rented that home, the home would pay you an income—this would make your second home an asset.

Chapter 14 Workbook
From Budget Avoidance to Budget Mastery

Motivation Boost
Link Between Budgeting and Happiness

Here is an absolute truth I have learned through education, teaching and practical experience: In the end, you will live your life frugally! You will either budget and create savings that will significantly improve all aspects of your life in the future or live frugally because you spent too much money and are now trying to remain financially afloat. Budgeting and living frugally is inevitable either way! Since that is the case, why not make living frugally count for something by creating a future life of financial abundance?

Budgeting and using your budget to analyze and prioritize your spending can get you more of whatever you desire, not less. A 2019 study showed that those who had more money were happier and had greater peace of mind than those who lived with minimal financial means.[11] Another study involving several countries demonstrated that increasing your assets (investments) and decreasing debt over time leads to greater life satisfaction.[12] Additionally, people with more financial resources were substantially happier than those who only had low debt and were missing the wealth component. This same study also noted a link between unhappiness, depression, and debt—although they could not say which came first, the depression or the debt.[13] Simply put, people were happier and more satisfied with their lives when they had less debt and more financial assets (investments) to generate additional income.

Action Step 1

Gather Info for a Budget

Budgets are usually created to track or control one month's worth of spending. Some budgets can be used to project spending and income for a year for analysis, but most budgets are based on monthly income and expenses.

1. Use either a spreadsheet on your computer or use a financial journal if you'd rather write it out. Only you are going to see this budget, so there is no advantage to "fudging" any numbers.
2. Gather up your income statements for a month's period. This includes payroll stubs or any other cash inflow like a 1099 (for contract work) and record this amount and total it.
3. Gather all your monthly bills and list all your regular monthly bills like rent, utility, car payments, loan payments, etc.
4. You likely don't know how much you spend on variable items like eating out, something to drink during the day, groceries, etc. Record your daily spending for at least couple of months. I use "notes" app on my phone, but there are plenty of specialized apps to help you record your daily expenses. It may take a couple of months to get a handle on how much you are spending in these various categories.
5. Don't expect perfection. Life happens, and things change.

Action Step 2

Choosing a Budget Type

Zero-based budgeting: You give every dollar you earn a specific job. You assign your income to either pay a priority monthly bill like rent, debt repayment or even savings. After assigning all your dollars a job, you should have zero left at the end of each month. There are several good apps to help with this budget.

The envelope system: After all regular monthly bills are paid and money is put into your savings, the rest of the money (in cash) is divided up into specifically labeled envelops for various household uses. This budget provides some flexibility, as money can be transferred from one envelope to another.

Cash only: To prevent credit card usage from getting out of hand and running up crippling, high-interest debt, all bills are paid with cash. This method is usually paired with the envelope system. All checks and cards are eliminated, as it is strictly a cash system.

Credit card only: This is the budget I use, but I do not recommend this budget for most people. My wife and I have categories on a spreadsheet to represent our budget allocations. All bills (even our house payments) are paid with a cash-back credit card. The credit card returns 3% to 5% back to us in cash or payment credit, depending on which category we spend our money in.

We do pay a significant annual credit card fee, but since we use it for everything, we actually make quite a bit of money using this system. This method is convenient in that we pay only one monthly bill. The entire credit card balance is automatically paid out of our checking account. We do not carry a balance on this credit card or any other card. If we did, the interest rate would be so high it would defeat the purpose of using this method.

We can review, categorize and analyze every dime we spend with our spreadsheet. This practice allows us, through analyzing our monthly expenses, to keep our expenses relatively low. If we have mistakes in spending, we have enough resources to cover our overage. Most people, unfortunately, do not have enough resources to cover unexpected expenses, which is why I do not recommend this budget. Also, most people tend to spend more if they use a credit card, which has been repeatedly proven by studies. We have been doing this for so long, however, we are goal, not spending, focused.

Action Step 3

Reduce Budget Anxiety

A. Automate your regular monthly bills (needs category). Automate your savings by direct deposit each paycheck. This only leaves your wants category to manage. This is a much smaller task that will create much less stress.

B. Focus on the positive. At least you are dealing with your situation, whatever it might be. No matter how bad it is, you can't go to jail for poor budget management. Even millionaires go broke and have to start all over again! Even if the situation is unsalvageable and you file for bankruptcy, you can overcome it in time. People have gotten rich after going bankrupt, as we saw in a previous motivational boost.

People feel like failures when they do poorly with their finances, but I know from being a financial coach that poor financial performance is the actually the norm and not the exception. Don't bother with feelings of shame or failure, just skip that step and move on to creating prosperity in your life.

Action Step 4

Lower Your Bills

Did you know you can frequently negotiate a lower rate from monthly providers and thereby lower your fixed costs? For example, utility companies like gas, electric, cable, internet providers and cell phone companies can sometimes provide you with discounts on your monthly bill if you call them and request a lower bill. My wife excels at getting these discounts. She will call and request one, and more often than not, she gets a monthly discount from that month forward. If they say no she simply tries again in another couple of months. The service provider representatives' ability to provide discounts vary from month to month, so timing is everything.

Also with phone and streaming services, you might consider family plans that are sometimes cheaper than several independent plans.

Action Step 5

Fix Your Upside-Down Budget

Many people have a budget that is upside down (spend more than they bring in each month). If you have this budget situation (actually very common), there are three steps you can take:

1. Increase your income.
2. Decrease your spending.

3. Increase your income and decrease your spending.

These are the only three ways to remedy an upside-down budget.

Action Step 6

Reasons a Credit Rating is Important

- Hiring is at least partially based upon an applicant's credit score.
- Applicants with poor credit or no credit are rejected as renters.
- Applicants with bad credit or no credit cannot qualify for a mortgage loan.
- Both auto and homeowners' insurance rates are impacted by credit score.
- Auto loan interest rates and terms are better with good credit.
- Special banking services and privileges (better rates with lower fees) are given to customers with better credit.
- Monthly cell phone services are only given to those with good credit, otherwise it is pay as you go.
- Credit is used as a determinate for security clearances within our government.

Action Step 7

Crisis or Disaster Budget

When I create a crisis budget, I engage all the basic financial steps we've covered.

1. Goal setting: Solve the crisis ASAP
2. Income creation: I go about creating additional emergency/income.

3. Budgeting: Spending on anything nonessential to survival is halted until the debt is banished.

4. Saving: Direct whatever emergency savings I have to the problem and limit future savings until the problem is solved.

5. Investing: A couple of times, Lisa and I have temporarily stopped adding to our investing program to eliminate a wolf at our door.

6. Pay priority bills first.

7. Tell yourself repeatedly and often that you can do anything temporarily and this budget is temporary.

8. Work on staying calm (deep breathing) so you can analyze your situation and come up with solutions such as:

- Refinance debt to a lower interest rate.

- Create additional income.

- Stop all wants spending. The only spending allowed are essential to survival and maintaining your employment.

- Contact your bank to see if they have a credit or debt counselor on staff.

Action Step 8

Debt Payoff Methods

The most common method of debt reduction is the snowball method, where you attack the smallest debt balance first, then the next smallest debt balance on the next loan and so on.

The avalanche method is the next most common method. You attack the debt or loan with the highest interest rate first. After that is paid off, you then attack the loan with the next highest interest rate and so on.

The site undebtit.com provides you with a spreadsheet and a timetable (based on the data you enter) for each of these methods to compare results. It also includes an analysis of a hybrid method (snowball and avalanche combined). This site easily allows you to compare what-if scenarios.

Action Step 9

Debt Resources

1. Financial Counseling Association of America (FCAA)
2. National Foundation for Credit Counseling (NFCC)

Action Step 10

Medical Debt

Many bankruptcies are created by crushing medical debt. In a lot of those cases, the patient was insured, but the medical insurance did not pay enough to prevent a financial disaster. There are several ways to reduce the cost of the medical bills you owe, however.

The best plan (whenever it is possible to do so) is to contact the doctor's office, the hospital, the clinic, urgent care or even the medical laboratory prior to service being provided and negotiating the costs of the procedure(s) ahead of time. This is how you get the very best pricing. If you are uninsured or have minimal medical insurance, this is the time to bring this subject up. Many of these facilities have special (lower) billing for uninsured or underinsured patients.

After the debt has been incurred, contact the hospital's accounts payable or billing department. The billing department is usually staffed with people who want to help you if they can. You can ask them for access to any debt forgiveness or financial aid programs they might have, as some hospitals have a program for customers who meet certain income criteria. You can also ask about discounts for cash payment(s) or taking a reduced payment now as payment in full.

Of course, you can always set up a payment plan wherever you receive or received medical treatment. Ask for the office manager who may have a better understanding of how to help you work through your medical debt challenges.

Many insurance companies deny claims as a strategy to reduce their costs and push those costs onto you. Never accept an insurance denial. Appeal the denial immediately and don't let the time limits expire for your appeal. The time limits are how they prevail. They keep the limits tight for this exact reason. If your appeal is denied, then appeal again. I have seen my wife Lisa appeal the same denied medical bill several times with our medical insurance company. In the end, she almost always wins.

If you don't have someone as skilled as my wife at reducing medical bills, you can hire a medical billing advocate who knows the ins and outs of medical billing. Contact the Patient Advocate Foundation or do an internet search for medical billing advocates in your area. These advocates will have knowledge of programs to help you pay medical bills.

Finally, there is federal and state money set aside for uninsured or underinsured patients. Contact your state government for referrals to the appropriate programs.

You may be eligible for Medicaid or Medicare in the future. Health and Human Services determines who is eligible for those programs.

Chapter 15 Workbook
From Money Disaster to Financial Prosperity

Motivation Boost
Smart Quotes to Consider

"We cannot solve our problems with the same thinking we used when we created them." —Albert Einstein

"Wherever you go, there you are." —Anonymous

"Maybe it is not even achieving success that matters. Maybe the point is the growth you create within yourself on your journey." —Larry Faulkner

Action Step 1

Stop Doing These Things Today

- Stop creating debt that will be hard to pay off.
- Stop avoiding your budget.
- Stop judging yourself in such a brutal and harsh way.
- Stop taking your partner for granted.
- Stop thinking that failures and setbacks are the end of your goal(s).
- Stop deciding to play it safe rather than evolve and change.

- Stop expecting the world to stay the same.
- Stop engaging in relationships that make you unhappy.
- Stop thinking that when all your dreams finally come true, you will finally be happy. It doesn't work that way!

Action Step 2

Start Doing These Today

- Understand we all have problems and a past that could hold us back. You are not alone!
- Start forgiving yourself.
- Start reframing your painful past experiences.
- Recognize your inner potential.
- Start being honest with yourself and your significant other.
- Start trying to be more positive about life and your goals.
- Write down all your goals.

Action Step 3

Increase Your Net Worth

- Budget your income to maximize its use.
- Pay down your debt.
- Increase your monthly income.
- Reduce your spending.
- Work on lowering your debt-to-income ratio.
- Select a life purpose, and appropriate goals that support that purpose.
- Manage life problems that interfere with your forward progress.
- Create an appropriate financial knowledge base.
- Focus on the future.

CITATIONS

Introduction

[1] Carnegie, Dale. 1964. *How to Win Friends and Influence People*. New York: Simon and Schuster.

Chapter 1

[1] https://www.ncbi.nlm.nih.gov/pmc/articles/PMC3968319/

[2] https://bestmoneymoves.com/blog/2020/02/25/financial-stress-health-and-employee-wellness-in-2020/

[3] https://www.weforum.org/agenda/2015/09/can-money-buy-you-happiness/

[4] ibid, Best money moves.

[5] https://www.investmentnews.com/dont-give-up-on-financial-literacy-efforts-188046

[6] https://www.getrichslowly.org/why-financial-literacy-fails-and-what-to-do-about-it/

[7] https://www.td.org/insights/emotional-intelligence-is-key-to-our-success

[8] https://www.preventchildabuse.org/images/docs/anda_wht_ppr.pdf

[9] https://bit.ly/32Wtoz5

[10] Bohls, Michelle LMFP. (08/05/20 at 3:00 PM). Phone interview.

[11] ibid, Bohls

[12] ibid, Bohls

[13] ibid, Bohls

[14] https://www.moneyquotient.org/blog/self-efficacy-the-key-to-financial-well-being/

[15] https://acestoohigh.com/got-your-ace-score/

Chapter 2

[1] https://www.psychologytoday.com/us/blog/mind-over-money/201001/the-big-lie-about-personal-finance

[2] Klontz, Brad, Psy.D. and Ted Klontz, Ph.D., Mind Over Money (New York, Broadway Books, 2009), Chap. 1, Samsung Galaxy.

[3] ibid, Klontz

[4] https://www.cnbc.com/2019/11/27/redline-these-money-moves-if-you-want-to-raise-financially-smart-kids.html

[5] ibid, Bohls interview.

[6] https://www.psychologytoday.com/us/blog/mind-over-money/201001/the-big-lie-about-personal-finance

[7] ibid, Bohls interview.

[8] https://www.psychologytoday.com/us/blog/mind-over-money/201805/your-beliefs-about-the-rich-may-be-keeping-you-poor?fbclid=IwAR30g-qOb-bRDHdd9WnCvxU5cWwOqtLwKOFeTgITH7w5YRYBVIGOudKrfrRk

[9] https://www.wife.org/financial-problems-making-feel-stupid-scientists-figured.htm

Chapter 3

[1] Faulkner, Larry. *Messages From Your Future: The Seven Rules For Financial, Personal, and Professional Success* (Dayton, Ohio, Faulkner Integrated Tactics 2016).

[2] ibid, Faulkner, Messages.

[3] https://hbr.org/2018/03/what-breaking-the-4-minute-mile-taught-us-about-the-limits-of-conventional-thinking

[4] https://www.inc.com/geoffrey-james/what-goal-setting-does-to-your-brain-why-its-spectacularly-effective.html

[5] Tracy, Brian. *Goals: How To Get Everything You Want Faster Than You Ever Thought Possible.* New York, NY: MJF Books, 2010.

[6] ibid, geoffrey-james.

Chapter 4

[1] https://aleteia.org/2018/02/24/brain-science-explains-why-bad-habits-are-so-hard-to-break/

[2] Duhigg, Charles. *The Power of Habit.* (New York: Random House Trade Paperbacks, 2014). Chapter 1, Apple I-Phone.

[3] https://habitica.fandom.com/wiki/The_Habit_Loop

4 https://www.inc.com/melody-wilding/psychology-says-this-is-how-you-change-a-bad-habit-for-good.html

5 https://www.artofmanliness.com/articles/power-of-habits/

6 https://niklasgoeke.com/ways-to-break-bad-habits/

7 https://www.npr.org/2012/03/05/147192599/habits-how-they-form-and-how-to-break-them

8 https://www.lifehack.org/810887/how-to-break-a-habit

9 https://www.sciencealert.com/how-long-it-takes-to-break-a-habit-according-to-science

10 https://www.drlaurendeville.com/articles/how-to-get-motivated-and-change-habits/

11 https://www.psychologytoday.com/us/blog/the-power-prime/201201/personal-growth-motivation-the-drive-change

12 https://www.apa.org/helpcenter/financial-avoidance

Chapter 5

1 https://americanaddictioncenters.org/behavioral-addictions

2 https://www.psychologytoday.com/us/blog/mind-over-money/201001/do-you-have-money-disorder

3 https://ajp.psychiatryonline.org/doi/10.1176/ajp.2006.163.10.1806

4 https://www.marketwatch.com/story/half-of-americans-are-just-one-paycheck-away-from-financial-disaster-2019-05-16

Chapter 6

1 https://www.kiplinger.com/article/spending/t037-c032-s014-understanding-and-dealing-with-misers.html

2 Dickens, Charles, and Richard Kelly. 2003. *A Christmas Carol.* Peterborough, Ont: Broadview Press

3 https://www.psychologytoday.com/us/blog/the-theater-the-brain/201712/dickens-christmas-carol

Chapter 7

1 https://economictimes.indiatimes.com/wealth/plan/does-your-spouse-lie-to-you-about-money-heres-how-to-deal-with-financial-infidelity/articleshow/72413064.cms?from=mdr

² https://www.npr.org/2019/04/29/716452865/keeping-money-se-crets-from-each-other-financial-infidelity-on-the-rise

³ https://www.psychologytoday.com/us/blog/when-kids-call-the-shots/201709/how-avoiding-conflict-escalates-conflict-in-relationships

⁴ https://www.psychologytoday.com/us/blog/mindful-anger/201708/4-ways-traumatic-childhood-affects-adult-relationships

⁵ ibid, Bohls

⁶ https://www.ml.com/the-financial-journey-of-modern-parenting.html

⁷ Faulkner, Larry. *Messages From Your Future: The Seven Rules For Financial, Personal, and Professional Success* (Dayton, Ohio, Faulkner Integrated Tactics 2016).

⁸ Faulkner, Larry. *The Illustrated Guide to Financial Independence.* (Austin, Texas, Faulkner Integrated Tactics, 2020).

Chapter 8

¹ Bohls, Michelle LMFP. (08/05/20 at 3:00 PM). Phone interview.

² ibid, Bohls

³ https://bit.ly/3clyyJJ

⁴ ibid, Googlebooks

⁵ ibid, Bohls

⁶ https://cpa-moms.com/why-you-are-underearning-and-how-to-stop/

⁷ https://www.marieforleo.com/2013/12/money-mindset/

⁸ https://www.inc.com/angelina-zimmerman/discover-the-7-key-traits-of-an-abundant-mindset.html

⁹ https://www.thecut.com/article/why-youre-not-making-enough-money.html

¹⁰ https://www.underearnersanonymous.org/wp-content/uploads/2018/11/Underearning-and-Thinking.pdf

¹¹ https://www.cheatsheet.com/money-career/biggest-money-problems-that-could-kill-your-marriage.html/

¹² Stanny, Barbara. Overcoming Underearning: A Five-Step Plan to a Rich Life. (New York, New York, Collins, c2005).

¹³ https://www.psychologytoday.com/us/blog/quantum-leaps/201907/how-re-write-your-past-narrative

14 https://www.mayoclinic.org/healthy-lifestyle/stress-management/in-depth/positive-thinking/art-20043950

15 https://www.inc.com/chris-winfield/want-to-be-rich-change-your-money-story.html

Chapter 9

1 https://www.nysscpa.org/news/publications/nextgen/nextgen-article/survey-77-percent-of-americans-stressed-over-finances-012820

2 https://mint.intuit.com/blog/financial-literacy/financial-statistics/

3 https://www.psychologytoday.com/files/attachments/34772/money-beliefs-and-financial-behaviors-development-the-klontz-money-script-inventory-jft-2011.pdf

4 https://www.moneybearcoaching.com/blog/2019/8/19/4-types-of-money-avoidance-revealed

5 https://www.psychologytoday.com/us/blog/loaded/201904/the-ostrich-effect

6 ibid, psychologytoday.com/ostrich-effect.

7 https://abcnews.go.com/GMA/story?id=843920&page=1

8 https://newprairiepress.org/cgi/viewcontent.cgi?article=1009&context=jft

9 https://sapience.com.au/blog/avoidant-money-beliefs

10 https://www.psychologytoday.com/us/blog/change-your-mind-change-your-money/201807/change-your-mind-change-your-money

11 https://psychlabs.ryerson.ca/caplab/why-vs-how-the-role-of-abstract-and-concrete-thinking-in-anxiety-and-depression-by-jenna-vieira/

12 https://www.ncbi.nlm.nih.gov/pmc/articles/PMC5446163/

13 ibid, ncbi.pmc/articles/PMC5446163

14 https://www.psychologytoday.com/us/blog/the-science-behind-behavior/202004/how-anxiety-affects-our-personal-finances

15 https://positivepsychology.com/goal-setting-psychology/

16 https://savology.com/6-benefits-of-financial-planning

17 Stanley, Thomas J, Ph.D. and William D. Danko, Ph.D. The Millionaire Next Door (New York, RosettaBooks LLC), Table 3.6. Samsung Galaxy.

18 https://www.psychologytoday.com/us/blog/change-your-mind-change-your-money/201810/how-train-your-brain-save-money

Chapter 10

1 https://www.verywellmind.com/the-benefits-of-optimism-3144811

2 Seligman, Martin E. PH.D. Learned Optimism: How To Change Your Mind And Your Life, 2nd ed. (New York, NY, Vintage Books, A Division of Random House Inc., 2006), Chapter 1, pages 2-17, Samsung Galaxy.

3 ibid, Seligman.

4 ibid, Seligman.

5 ibid, Seligman.

6 https://positivepsychology.com/learned-helplessness-seligman-theory-depression-cure/

7 ibid, positivepsychology.

8 ibid, positivepsychology.

9 https://www.psychologytoday.com/us/basics/learned-helplessness

10 https://www.verywellmind.com/learned-helplessness-in-children-1066762

11 ibid, learned-hleplessness.

12 ibid, learned-hleplessness.

13 https://optimisticbrain.com/stuff-to-read/optimistic-reframing/

14 https://www.verywellmind.com/how-to-use-a-positive-reframe-for-stress-management-3144885

15 ibid, verywellmind, positive reframe.

16 https://www.optforoptimism.com/optimism/optimismresearch.pdf

17 http://ijepr.org/panels/admin/papers/159ij12.pdf

18 http://glennstearns.com/about/

19 https://www.abc4.com/community/gmu-sponsored/undercover-billionaire/

20 https://www.verywellmind.com/how-to-be-optimistic-4164832

21 ibid, Seligman. chapter 12.

22 https://www.optforoptimism.com/optimism/optimismresearch.pdf

Chapter 11

1 https://www.psychologytoday.com/us/blog/the-new-resilience/201509/sense-awe-and-life-purpose-increases-your-mental-health

2 https://www.psychologytoday.com/us/blog/mind-over-money/201309/living-purpose

3 https://www.psychologytoday.com/us/blog/the-new-resilience/201509/sense-awe-and-life-purpose-increases-your-mental-health

4 ibid, the-new-resilience

5 https://www.tandfonline.com/doi/abs/10.1080/01488376.2014.896851 3

6 www.forbes.com/sites/alicegwalton/2017/07/10/the-science-of-giving-back-how-having-a-purpose-is-good-for-body-and-brain/#1b1001466146

7 https://www.ncbi.nlm.nih.gov/pmc/articles/PMC5408461/

8 https://www.ncbi.nlm.nih.gov/pmc/articles/PMC5408461/

9 https://www.apa.org/helpcenter/willpower-fact-sheet

10 https://www.verywellmind.com/tips-for-finding-your-purpose-in-life-4164689

11 https://qz.com/1310792/the-secret-to-a-meaningful-life-is-simpler-than-you-think/

Chapter 12

1 Siebold, Steve. How Rich People Think. (London House Press, 2010), Chapter 15, pages 32-33, Samsung Galaxy.

2 https://www.willistowerswatson.com/en-US/News/2020/02/despite-improvement-in-their-financial-wellbeing-US-workers-remain-worried

3 https://www.psychologytoday.com/us/blog/i-hear-you/201907/why-are-millennials-so-anxious-and-unhappy

4 https://www.srdc.org/media/199920/fcac-full-report-on-financial-confidence-en.pdf

5 https://www.sciencedirect.com/science/article/pii/S016748701500094X

6 https://hbr.org/2020/09/does-more-money-really-makes-us-more-happy

7 https://www.northwesternmutual.com/who-we-are/

8 https://www.latimes.com/archives/la-xpm-2004-dec-12-me-then12-story.html

Chapter 13

1 Faulkner, Larry. *Messages From Your Future: The Seven Rules For Financial, Personal, and Professional Success* (Dayton, Ohio, Faulkner Integrated Tactics 2016).

2 https://www.thebalancesmb.com/the-history-of-franchising-1350455

3 https://www.inc.com/amanda-abella/want-to-become-a-millionaire-create-multiple-streams-of-income.html

4 https://www.apa.org/advocacy/socioeconomic-status/scarcity-fact-sheet.pdf

5 ibid, APA. Socioeconomic-status.

6 Siebold, Steve. How Rich People Think. (London House Press, 2010), Chapters 1-100, Samsung Galaxy.

7 https://www.psychologytoday.com/us/blog/click-here-happiness/201904/15-ways-build-growth-mindset

8 https://www.forbes.com/sites/ashleystahl/2016/05/11/how-self-worth-affects-your-salary/?sh=ea68f1077fa0

9 https://www.urbanbalance.com/unearthing-the-link-between-money-self-esteem-and-happiness/

10 https://bpspsychub.onlinelibrary.wiley.com/doi/abs/10.1348/0963179041752646

11 https://www.healthaffairs.org/do/10.1377/hpb20180817.901935/full/.

12 https://www.nytimes.com/2020/01/16/science/rich-people-longer-life-study.html

13 Kiyosaki, Robert T., and Sharon L. Lechter. 1998. Rich Dad, Poor Dad: What the Rich Teach Their Kids About Money That the Poor and Middle Class Do Not! Paradise Valley, Ariz: TechPress.

14 https://www.richdad.com/what-are-assets-and-liabilities

Chapter 14

1 https://getmoneyrich.com/pay-yourself-first/

2 https://www.debt.com/statistics/

3 https://www.thecut.com/2017/05/the-annoying-psychology-of-why-you-cant-stick-to-a-budget.html

4 https://www.apa.org/topics/personality/willpower-finances

5 https://www.apa.org/topics/stress/money

6 ibid, www.thecut.com, annoying-psychology.

7 ibid, www.thecut.com, annoying-psychology.

8 https://www.psychologytoday.com/us/blog/good-thinking/201306/how-boost-your-willpower

9 https://www.businessinsider.com/the-4-biggest-financial-fears-2012-10

10 http://www.wipsociology.org/2018/10/29/income-and-wealth-are-not-highly-correlated-here-is-why-and-what-it-means/

11 https://www.cnbc.com/2019/10/10/study-millennials-who-buy-less-and-save-more-are-happier.html

12 https://www.startribune.com/saving-money-makes-you-happier-here-s-proof/454801593/

13 ibid, startribune.com/saving.

Also by Larry Faulkner

The Illustrated Guide to Financial Independence

Message From Your Future: The Seven Rules for Financial, Personal and Professional Success

About Larry Faulkner

Larry Faulkner is an award-winning author of *The Illustrated Guide To Financial Independence*, a #1 Amazon Bestseller. He is also a self-made millionaire and has personally made the journey he writes about in his books and articles. Larry is a Certified Financial Education Instructor and teaches classes regularly to diverse groups of people from prisoners in jail, all the way to groups of interested professionals such as doctors, lawyers and police officers.

Larry now lives in Austin, Texas with his wife Lisa, of 30 years. The couple is financially independent and they love the life they have designed and built together. One of their passions is travel and the couple enjoys travel adventures all over the US and abroad.

About Michelle Bohls, LMFT

In her private practice in Austin, Michelle Miller Bohls, LMFT specializes in working with interpersonal relationships in adult process groups and with couples. Michelle has been deeply fascinated with our psychological relationship with money—who is challenged to make it, save it, or spend it.

Michelle is part of the International Imago Faculty where she trains counselors and coaches worldwide on how to facilitate safe conversations with couples, groups, and in organizations—including safe conversations about money.

Made in the USA
Columbia, SC
06 March 2022